CURIOUS INCIDENTS
IN THE GARDEN
AT NIGHT-TIME

The Fantastic Story of the
Disappearing Night

Allan Shepherd

Centre for
Alternative
Technology
Publications

Allan Shepherd
© October 2005
Centre for Alternative Technology,
Machynlleth, Powys, SY20 9AZ UK
Tel. 01654 705950   Fax. 01654 702782
email. info@cat.org.uk   website. www.cat.org.uk

Illustrations: Chloë Ward
Cover Art: Clare Maynard
claremaynard@ukartists.com
Edited by Caroline Oakley and Hele Oakley
Design: Graham Preston

ISBN 1-90217-525-5

1 2 3 4 5 6 7 8 9 10

Printed in Great Britain by Cambrian Printers,
Aberystwyth, 01970 627111
on Cyclus Offset paper, made from 100% post consumer waste.

Published by CAT Publications, CAT Charity Ltd. Registered charity no. 265239

The manufacturing process reduces the need for landfill sites and the minimal production waste is recycled.

This book is for my sister Hazel, who has always been there for me with practical and moral support whenever I've needed it. Thank you for all your love. And for being you.

And for Sue and Marly, for showering me with brightness in dark winter hours. Thank you for all your encouragement and love.

Acknowledgements

I would like to thank Chloë Ward for her gardening advice and for bringing the moth collectors illustrations to life, and Clare Maynard for painting us such a beautiful front cover. I would also like to thank Russel Jones of RSPB reserve Ynis Hir, Joe Ironside of the Institute of Biological Sciences at the University of Wales, Aberystwyth, Anne Marie Carty, and my friends and colleagues in the publications and mail order departments at The Centre for Alternative Technology: to Graham Preston for the beautiful way in which he has designed this book, Hele Oakley, for playing a perfect hand throughout and Hazel Jones for all her support and enthusiasm. It is much appreciated.

One day there will be no night. Or, I should say, on one side of our planet there will be no night. On the other there will be nothing but night. On this day the earth will finally stop revolving on its own axis. It will not undertake some cosmic emergency breaking procedure. We don't have to worry about that. It will simply wind down, at a rate of two milliseconds per century, getting infinitesimally slower with each passing year, as it has done for the past four and a half billion years, until it turns no more.

Some millions of years before the world finally stops we will have to get off. A planet revolving with such little enthusiasm will be an inhospitable place to live. If there was someone alive to record the passing of this last day, to note every crushingly unpleasant moment, they would have to live through millennia to do so.

1

Mrs Jones of Bethlehem, Wales, has often wished for a few extra hours in the day, but even she would run out of porcelain statuettes to arrange and dust given a thousand years to complete the task. If she knows about the rotational forces dragging her days through another year she is not letting on. Questions of astrological coincidence are not her cup of tea.

Standing on the chipped, cracked, concrete step to her back door, in the spotty lamp-lit twilight of Christmas Eve, Mrs Jones calls her cat Megan to evening prayer at her little bowl. She rolls the word Megan out like a tenpin bowling ball. The 'e' is stretched into an 'ay', the 'a' into an 'er'. The word gathers so much pace as she comes to the end, the final 'r' could knock down skittles on its own. To top the chant off she loops onto the end a rising exclamation mark. 'Maygerrrrn! Maygerrrn!'

The whole village knows when it's time for Megan's supper. Only Mr Jones, sitting in the back room inside the house, cannot hear the call. Hearing aids are handy things for the deaf. They can be turned down as well as up.

Mrs Jones is fearful of the night, and even though she is on her own step, her fear of being alone in the dark adds some anxiety to her call: 'Maygerrrn! Maygerrrrn!'

On Christmas Eve, what cat wouldn't respond to such a loving call? Sure enough, Megan, all silver fluff and soft paws, pushes across the wintered turf of her lawn, clouding her eyes with warm damp mists as she goes. The light has gone from the day and the pupils of her eyes are not slits any more but wide pools. Like the two wife'd baker of Llaregub, Megan has two types of cell in her eye – one for the day and one for the night. The rod cells are the late shift workers of the eye, filling up each night with visual purple, a vision-enhancing chemical. The cone cells are the cells of daytime and of colour. In Mrs Jones's case they are the cells of strawberry jam and needlecraft. Without them, the Cambrian poppies in her garden would not seem so appealingly yellow.

Mrs Jones will never be a nocturnal hunter. Not like the owl, whose eyes contain only rods. Nor though should she be as timid as the rodless, night blind chicken, who has good biological reasons for returning to the hen house every night. But then again, Megan, who has two thousand times as many rods as Mrs Jones, will still never fish dark seas with a dolphin.

2

A lone cyclist, travelling towards the village along the strolling twist of a road that passes by Mrs Jones's terrace, sees the glow from his front light reflecting in glass cat's-eyes. Cocooned in waterproofs, hat and gloves, he is as cosy as the moth larvae he is thinking about as he peddles home.

Tonight there are no cars on the road, no clouds and no moon yet, and no light at all between the moth collector and the rest of the Earth's galaxy. He switches off his front bike light and pitches his head up, sensing the direction of the road from the tops of the trees that line it and funnel his view toward the sky. The road is flat, so there is little danger. He pedals slowly and has time to take it all in.

On a clear night like this, with his head full of wonder and his heart full of oxygen, the moth collector sees in the stars the whole history of humanity. He sees the myths and legends of the explanation of the stars. He sees the great empires of Greece and Rome, whose scholars painted dot-to-dot gods on the night sky and held greatness as a gift from them. He sees Egyptian pyramids and Mayan temples lined up with stars. He sees the Indian creator of the myth of Prajapati (or Orion as we call it), the lord of creatures who fathered twenty-seven daughters and was shot by a great belt of an arrow for seducing one of them.

He sees science in the stars. He sees the third century mathematician, Ptolemy, scratching onto leather parchment 1,000 stars in forty-eight constellations. He sees Copernicus, a thousand years later, waiting for a clear night like this to climb the turrets of Poland's Frauenberg Cathedral and chart the skies with nothing more than a few primitive instruments and his naked eyes. He sees Galileo building his first telescope, kept under house arrest by the Catholic Inquisition for proving Copernicus's proposition that the Earth went round the sun. He sees that other great heretic, Martin Luther, founder of the

Protestant faith, protesting angrily of Copernicus, 'The fool will turn the whole art of astronomy inside out! As the Holy Scripture reports, Joshua ordered the sun to stand still and not the Earth.'

He sees novels and poems and music in the stars. And art. He sees Van Gogh and Shakespeare. He sees James Joyce, walking out of his Dublin study in search of a phrase and finding it under a 'heaventree of stars hung with humid night-blue fruit'. He sees Harper Lee and Truman Capote sneaking into the backyard of the frightened, and frightening, Boo Radley, under a whole orchard of night-blue fruit.

And for every star above him and every beat of a pedal turned beneath him he hears a song. Stars to wish on, stars that fall, stars to catch and put in your pocket. And all the moons you could ever want: blue moons, new moons, harvest moons, moons of love, moon glows, moon rivers, sonatas and Sinatras:

'Fly me to the moon and let me wish upon the stars.

'Take me up to Jupiter, Venus and Mars.

'In other words say I do. In other words, say I love you.'

It takes a while to shake this last song from his head but when he does he concentrates on the rhythm of his own movement. The regular beat of rotation and breath. Rotation and breath... Rotation and breath... Click... The sound of the wheel. Rotation, breath, click... And the sound of the swoosh of air on his coat. Rotation, breath, click, swoosh... And on.

During the first few hundred thousand years of the universe space was just a glowing plasma of chemical energy. There was no darkness, only light. After that the light went out, completely, and the universe entered a period of absolute darkness. This first cosmic night was 500 million years old when it ended. That's quite a night. And then, 14 billion years ago the nuclear fire of the first star ignited itself and somewhere in the universe a revolving piece of rock orbiting this first star experienced the first day and night.

This is the sort of thing the moth collector likes to dream about on a night like this. He likes to imagine himself travelling with the rest of the universe on the outward leg of a journey towards some undefined destiny, a tiny particle in the middle of a giant explosion that has been going on for fourteen-and-a-half billion years. An explosion that started with the biggest bang from the smallest amount of matter ever imagined and ends... well, who knows where it will end. This doesn't matter to him. The Earth will stop rotating before that happens; humankind will depart before the earth stops rotating and the moth collector will stop dreaming before then.

But a night like this is a pitch at eternity.

The moth collector's mind drifts to the memory of a play he saw about the mythic birth of the universe. The show was an unrelenting, thrashing, calamitous riot of a play until two actors took to the stage, naked but for two cardboard stars.

The two naked stars demanded silence. But they couldn't decide what kind of silence to have. They went through the options: twenty or more types of silence, each one representing a different moment in a person's life.

The moth collector thinks about what sort of silence he would like to hear. He remembers that during one long period of Earth's natural history, not a living thing made a vocal noise. There were no barks or hoots, or laughs, or croaks, or sighs. No bird song, no howl, no roar or scream. Nothing. There were animals, but none of them needed to express themselves vocally in anyway. They had not even evolved the mechanisms needed to vocalise feeling. Even day and night sounded the same.

The moth collector stops his bike, gets off, sits on the side of the road and waits. An owl hoots three or four times. But then it stops and the world stills itself for just a moment. Long enough for him to hear the type of silence that existed 330 million years ago. Nothing but a low continuous hum. The ancient silence of a stream. Brought to our planet on the backs of comets, water is the white background noise to all life.

And then he sneezes.

He blows his nose, gets back on to his bike and carries on to the village. As he moves under the first street light all but the brightest stars vanish. The magic has gone and his thoughts turn to other things.

Cycling through the village he sees smokers stubbing out butt-ends in the village hall car park and a man retrieving his keys from the lip of a storm drain outside the Black Lion. Lucky... The house is cold when he gets in. He sets about lighting a fire, and drops a match as his neighbour, Mrs Jones, starts up again.

'Maygerrrn! Maygerrrn!'

Megan has been distracted by something and the call is impatient.

3

Megan has picked out a tiny flutter of wings in the night sky and, unsure in the dim light whether it is a bird or a bat, follows it. The little object moves too slowly to be either and Megan loses interest.

If only the moth collector was here and not Megan. This little object would be of great interest to him. It is a moth, a very rare moth indeed, an Orange Upperwing[1]. Last seen by human eyes in 1994, thought possibly to be extinct, and now here, in his neighbour's garden.

The Orange Upperwing works hard for its flight. Every time it raises and lowers its wings it swivels them too: a tiny adjustment that creates a vortex of swirling air beneath its body. The vortex pushes air downwards underneath the wing and lifts the moth up. It is a constant effort, and very soon the Orange Upperwing needs to rest. It grounds itself on an oak tree belonging to Mr Jones, planted the first week of his marriage to replace the one he used to make his wedding bed.

This little moth is not particularly spectacular: a fleck of honey-glazed orange fibre on a highway of bark, distinguished from other moths of its type by four light orange spots and a pencil thin dark orange band scratched across its wings.

Usually the Orange Upperwing rests between mid-November and February, hardly stirred by need or enemy. It stays the winter quiet amongst dry oak leaves, if it can find them; a bellyful of autumn nectar burning cautiously through short days and long nights. Kindled awake by the unusual warmth of this Christmas Eve night, the Orange Upperwing finds there are no sallow catkins to keep its ghostly fire alive. Though the Orange Upperwing thinks it is time to start going about its spring tasks, the plants do not agree.

The day has been mild – but still cold enough for Megan. Barely stopping to push her tail up along the seam of Mrs Jones's stocking, she passes into the dry warmth of the house. As she moves down the hallway she licks away the steam from her nostrils and inhales the scents of smoke and giblets. Mr Jones sees the cat and resets his hearing aid.

Megan leaves dirty paw prints on the newly vacuumed carpet but Mrs Jones doesn't notice. She has other animals on her mind, and one more outdoor task to perform. A plate of bacon rinds, cut from the sausage wraps of tomorrow's turkey dinner, must be trimmed for the bird table.

With a sigh to the stars, Mrs Jones returns to the cosy love of her cat and her husband when the task is done, and with thoughts of her youngest grandson's smile in her head walks straight over the messy cat prints, picking up tiny particles of earth as she goes. With each new step she spreads an invisible mosaic of earth fragments on the microscopic fabric stalks, which, in the tiny forest world of the shag-pile, make excellent food for mites. And so the cat prints become so much dust in the pile, to be hoovered up, along with the mites and the springtails, in the weekly clean.

4

There comes a point in the day when the human body clock starts to change the way we feel. For Mr Jones that moment has come. His body is enjoying the sedative qualities of the chemical melatonin. The melatonin is triggered from deep within a part of his brain called the suprachiasmatic nucleus, or SCN for short. It has been switched on by a series of events in his body brought on by the falling light levels.

The brain never sees the light of day directly. Instead it receives coded messages sent to it by tiny impulses from the eyes. Our minds never see the world as it is, only what our eyes interpret for us.

When light levels fall, the cells in our retinas detect this change and tell the SCN that it's time to start feeling sleepy. A fraction of a milligram of melatonin can induce sleep, and the brain times its release to peak between one and two in the morning. Most of us fall asleep before that point is reached, somewhere between eleven and twelve. Mr Jones will probably fall asleep some time before that.

Mrs Jones switches off the light in the kitchen where she has just washed bacon grease off the plate and returns to her comfy chair. She picks up two-thirds of a home knitted scarf and smiles as Mr Jones reads, as he does every night, from the Bible.

'"Let there be light," and there was light. God saw that the light was good, and God separated the light from the darkness. God called the light Day, and the darkness He called Night.'

The room is roasted by 350 million year old anthracite, the last type of coal to be dug from a Welsh mine. Mr Jones puffs out tobacco smoke like a dragon and reads with the melodic fervour of a piper in a valley fog. The dense atmosphere of the room is filled with the rising fumes of coarse burnt tobacco and a warm hurricane of aromas from the stewed juices of the Christmas Eve roast. Mr and Mrs Jones revel in the familiarity and the winter warmth of their life.

5

Conquering melatonin with cold air and wistfulness, the moth collector stands alone amidst the dead skeleton of his garden. The branches of the trees scrape cold harmonies, and bark, from one another. He longs for summer.

The moth collector's garden is not particularly big. Just a rough, crooked square of flat ground interrupted by the elevations of plants and a single ordinary looking wooden shed. On three sides, the garden is closed by a roughly shorn hedge of old coppiced oak and beech. In places, common ivy[2] has scaffolded itself around the hedge, its own branches so thick and heavy that birds nest in its folds. In other seasons, a wall of leaves shield an emerald city of chrysalis and caterpillar. In the autumn, adult moths take nectar from yellow-green flowers.

In other parts of the hedge the vines of honeysuckle[3] take over, but do not cling with the wanton passion of ivy. They push away from the hedge in fickle displays of independence, pushing out to the sky. In a breeze, their tips shake and quiver. Out of the wind they are as still and calm as ancient crags. In places, the oak and beech are little more than a prop for the sprawling tangled stems of common jasmine[4]. Its white star flowers are so bright and alien in the acquiescent trees beneath, that they appear like snowflakes in a desert.

On the fourth side of the garden, concrete steps and slate walls hold the bulging garden in like a corset, stopping it sliding into the houses below. In places, the fat of the land has slipped through tears in the fabric. Cambrian poppy[5] seeds lodge in thin crusts of soil and produce flowers that puncture the hard grey mass with the colour of sunlight. To the left-hand side of the steps the moth collector allows the stalks of gourds[6] to tumble over the wall, the summer fruit looking like so many humpty-dumptys on a string. Each one has a name more descriptive than its neighbour: the bottle gourd, the club, powder horn, the dipper, the penguin. At night the moth collector watches the paper-thin flowers open wide until they are almost bent over backwards like gymnasts.

When he climbs up to his garden he is Michelangelo climbing to the chapel ceiling.

The moth collector's garden is a tribute to creation and the night. To rod cells and melatonin. To the moon and moths. Every plant in it has some quality brought out by darkness. Whether it is the opening of a flower bud, the release of scent, or the illumination of a certain type of bold whiteness only really visible when colour is banished from the eye.

How the moth collector longs for summer darkness. Then he can suspend himself over the warm palette of his dreams. Climbing into a hammock to let the universe drift over him. Floating in fragrance. Night scents rising from every quarter. The white petals of bird cherry[7] falling on his face. Watching constellations move across the sky as the hours pass. Studying the moon, or just as likely the contour of a favourite plant soaked to the skin in its light.

If he is in a playful mood he will tip his head over the back end of the hammock, as if trailing the ends of his hair in water, and look north towards garden apple trees and the cloaked, wooded shores of oak and beech in the woodland behind. When the wind raises a commotion in the garden, with dreamy half-closed eyes, he watches the upside down sway of white foxgloves[8]. Sometimes they brush the lowest fruit on the trees. Still young apples bob on the crested waves of his imagination, a flotilla of globes drift towards him: warm, moist fruits of some make-believe Arabian sea.

And then, coming up for air, he will throw his body forwards to the front of his boat and cannon looks across an open sky. He has an armoury of gazes, glances, scans and long hard stares to see the world in every way. His garden is a rippling sea of latitude…

A free kingdom.

Bedded in drifts beneath the bird cherry the almond-scented white bell flowers of the twin flower[9] bob too. When the moon is rich and full, the moth collector allows his eyes to glaze over and for a moment they sparkle like stars.

6

If he has a friend to share his hammock, as well as his enthusiasm, the moth collector tells them the story of the first night on Earth. When the world was just a bubbling mass of molten rock. When sunlight lit the Earth's surface for the first time. When day arrived to define night.

He tells them that the first night was over in a few minutes, but in those few minutes the earth travelled the same distance on its axis as it does now in twelve hours. He tells them that the earth travelled at such a pace that, if any life form had been there to witness the event, the stars would appear to them to pass through the night sky like comets.

What an amazing stroke of luck it is, he tells his friend, that only a short while after this first night our planet gained the right sized magnet of a moon to pull the Earth into an acceptable pace of rotation. And that without the moon there would be no life because Earth would be all wobble and spin. Wobble and spin. And moss grows slowly on a rolling, wobbling, spinning stone.

When he speaks the moth collector does so with urgency, each sentence pushed on by an unquenchable desire to communicate his passion.

'So, boom, a massive meteorite hits the Earth. The collision throws huge chunks of molten rock into space which spin together to form one new ball of rock. The two balls of rock that are the Earth and its moon exert a strong magnetic force on each other. This magnetism slows the Earth down and forces the moon to orbit the earth, which at this point has an atmosphere like an exhaust. Made up of carbon dioxide and various other noxious gases. It takes 300,000 years for the first life-form to emerge. A tiny cell of chlorophyll, which splits carbon from carbon dioxide and breathes out oxygen. And that's all there is for billions of years. Billions of these cells, just splitting carbon dioxide into carbon and oxygen. And letting the oxygen go. For three-and-a-half billion years this is the only thing that happens on Earth. No walking, no talking, no seeing, no hearing, no fighting, no eating.'

'No sex?'

'No sex, they just join together and break off. It's a totally asexual, non-violent world. Cells just amalgamate, or absorb one another. They start to form larger organisms. Single cells join together into communities – mats of blue-green slime – and these grow into towers of slime. Getting bigger and bigger until the oceans are full of forests of towers of slime. And the atmosphere is full of oxygen. Enough oxygen for cells to form more complicated structures. Structures that move. Structures that have to eat to get energy.'

'When is this, by the way?'

'About 525 million years ago.'

'About?' She thinks it is quite a precise estimate.

He continues, hardly missing a beat. 'It's like that Orson Wells speech in *The Third Man*.'

'The one at the top of the Ferris wheel.'

'Yes! You know it?'

'In Italy for thirty years under the Borgias they had warfare, terror, murder, and bloodshed, but they produced Michelangelo, Leonardo da Vinci and the Renaissance.'

'Yes!'

'In Switzerland,' she carries on, 'they had brotherly love – they had 500 years of democracy and peace, and what did that produce?'

'The Cuckoo Clock.' They say this last part together and laugh.

She asks him how this relates to what he is saying.

'Well,' he replies, 'in three-and-a-half billion years of peaceful co-operation and photosynthetic passivity you get nothing but slime.'

16

'And in half a billion years of violence, gluttony and sex...?'

'You get the most beautiful colours the world has ever seen, the most elegant movement, the most fantastic sounds, the most curious shapes.'

He pauses to listen to her breathing.

And then continues.

'But the amazing thing is, no matter what happens in those 500 million years, nothing is ever so gloriously experimental and fantastic as that first explosive period of life. It only lasts a few million years, but by the end of it you have all the basic animal structures in place. It's like life decided what really worked then, and anything that happens afterwards is just tinkering. There's only one new phylum...'

'Ih...urh.' The moth collector's friend interrupts him with a noise that sounds like the wrong answer buzzer from *Family Fortunes*. ('"We asked you to name a type of bed. You said flowerbed. Our survey said, "Ih...urh."') 'You were doing so well. What's a phylum?'

'A phylum is a... Hang on a minute it's easier if I show you. Hold on to the hammock, I have to get out.'

'Where are you going?'

But he has already tumbled out of the hammock, splashed on to the mossy lawn beneath and set off across it on all fours, crawling like a child.

'I have to go and get my Memory Book from the shed.'

'Your what?' She calls out after him, the sound of her voice muffled by the cotton cloth of the hammock, which wraps itself around her as she sinks into the middle of it.

The moth collector can't hear her.

When he returns to the hammock he is carrying a red and black notebook. He climbs back in and starts flicking through the pages.

'My Memory Book. I kept it when I first started getting interested in moths. I wrote stuff down...'

'Cos you found it easier to remember.'

'You do that too?' He asks her.

'All the time.'

'And then it kind of grew and now its got all sorts of stuff in it. OK. Phylum. That would be about June 2000.' He started to flick through the pages. 'April, May.'

She is impressed. 'Very organised.'

'June. Started this on January 1st, 2000.' He flicked through some more pages. 'June 10th... Two new year's resolutions... June 14th. One to learn about moths. One to remember more. There we are, June 19th, 2000.'

He opens up at a page with a table containing two lists of names. Most of them are unfamiliar to her.

June 19th - Homo sapiens

Kingdom   Animalia
Phylum   Chordata
Class   Mammalia
Order   Primate
Family   Hominidae
Genus   Homo
Species   Homo sapiens

He explains the page to her. 'I wanted to learn how biologists categorised animals so I found this table that showed where humans fit into the great scheme of things. These are all the Latin words but I'll translate. Kingdom is obviously animal. Other kingdoms are plants, funghi… You can see below that level is phylum.'

'Yep.' She feels she is following it pretty well.

'Phyla are pretty big groups of animals.' He points to the word 'Chordata'. '*Chordata* are animals with a spinal chord. Grouped in here are various classes of animals like birds, mammals, amphibians, reptiles and so on. And then within that you get orders of species like primates, bats, whales.'

'So what makes a mammal a mammal?'

'At each level all the animals within a particular category have a defining feature that makes them the same as the other animals in the category. The defining feature of a mammal is that they all suckle their young. Mammals are then split again. *Hominidae* basically means two legged species, like us, although we're the only ones in this family that aren't extinct. And then you get more variations under that. Genus, and then species. We're *Homo sapiens*. So our genus is *Homo* and our species is *Homo sapiens*. We're different in some way · to *Homo erectus*, *Homo neanderthalensis*.'

'Neanderthal man?'

'Right. As I said, all other members of our genus and our family are extinct. We have to wait until we get to primates before we fit in anywhere. Here's another one, for an endangered species of British moth called *Jodia croceago*. Its common name is Orange Upperwing.'

June 21st - Jodia croceago

Kingdom	Animalia
Phylum	Anthropoda
Class	Insecta
Order	Lepidoptera
Family	Noctuidae
Genus	Arconictinae
Species	Jodia croceago

He carries on. 'So, in this chart *Arthropoda* means they have jointed legs but no backbone. This group includes the class *Insecta*, species with six legs, and centipedes, millipedes, spiders. *Lepidoptera* means creatures with scaled (lepis) wings (pteron). Basically, butterflies and moths. There's a huge number of species in this group. The only order with more is the beetles – or *Coleoptra* to give them their Latin name.'

'So what are the other phylum?'

'For that I will need another page.' The moth collector starts to flick through the book again.

She smiles, 'Don't worry I'll look at it later.'

They lean towards each other and kiss.

When they pull apart his cheeks are flushed.

'Anyway,' he stumbles on, 'it's all in the fossil record. Defining features of all the phyla that exist today can be found in fossils from that period, and then from that period through to now.'

He pauses for a minute to watch a shooting star.

Then he asks, 'Have you ever seen that Jimmy Stewart film, *It's a Wonderful Life*?'

'Just about every Christmas.'

'Well, you know that scene where George Bailey promises to lasso the moon for Mary?'

'"Buffalo girls won't you come out tonight. Come out tonight. Come out tonight. Buffalo girls won't you come out tonight. And dance by the light of the moon."'

'"What did you wish for when you threw that rock."'

They both laugh.

And he carries on. 'Well, with you I think it's the other way round. I think the moon lassoed you.'

'You lassooed me,' she replies, ' and don't you forget it. Moon or no moon.'

He picks up his Memory Book and looks over another page for the Orange Upperwing.

Orange Upperwing (Jodia croceago)

Used to be common. Historical distribution included Wiltshire, Oxfordshire, the West Midlands and the Isle of Wight. Recorded in fair numbers on the border of Surrey and West Sussex up until 1977 but last seen there in 1983. Also seen in Cornwall (1983), East Sussex (1984), North Hampshire (1992).

- Singletons seen in Aber Magwyr in 1955 and Llechryd in 1982.

- Last confirmed sighting - six individuals between 5th October and 4th November 1994 between Cardigan and Aberystwyth!

She reads the page too. 'Where does all this come from?'

'It's from a field guide. People like me going out every night counting moths.'

'So are you in this guide?'

'Me? No. If I see anything rare—'

'If you see an Orange Upperwing?'

'Yes. But that's unlikely.'

'Do you think it's extinct?'

'They're not usually officially called extinct until they've not been seen for fifty years. But even if we saw a living example it might be as good as extinct.'

'How come?'

'It may already have crossed the point of no return. Mathematicians call it the "absorbing barrier".'

'Absorbing barrier. That's a pretty clinical word for the loss of a species.'

'Yeah. I guess the damage has already been done by then. It's the point where a species can't absorb losses caused by ordinary chance events. When chance starts to dictate the future rather than some evolutionary survival strategy.'

'Explain.'

'Are you asking me to explain evolutionary theory?'

'I don't know. Am I?'

'I think you might be.'

'Can you?' She asks, almost hoping at this stage of the evening that he can't.

'No. Not all of it.'

'A bit of it then.'

'OK.'

'OK.' She agrees. 'But I think I need to get a little more comfortable for this one. Move your arm a bit.' She takes his arm and places it around her shoulder, so that her body tilts into his, and her head rests on his chest.

'OK. That's better. You may begin, sir.'

'How should I start?' It's a big subject to leap into. He finds his starting point when he sees a bat circling above them both.

'You know a bat uses sonar to hunt moths? And that moths are much slower than bats? On the face of it the moth doesn't have much of a chance. Bat sonar is incredible. It can tell the bat whether the insect it is hunting is soft bodied or hard bodied, how big it is, how far away, which direction it is heading. A moth can't fight back against that in any conventional way. So it has learnt how to hear the bat's sonar. But it doesn't learn this in any deliberate way. Natural selection just gets rid of a greater proportion of the ones that can't learn it.'

To the moth collector his friend sounds as though she is falling asleep. Her breast rises and falls gently against the side of his abdomen.

'OK.' He is distracted now and isn't sure whether she, or he, will make it to the end of his explanation.

'All animals have master control genes, hox genes, as they're known. They tell cells in an embryo what to do. You make an eye. You a leg. We need a wing here. But if a hox gene fails in some way, it can lose control of the other genes. The error may throw up a new body part or make some existing body part stronger or weaker, or alter colourings and so on. Or equally, the hox genes can send a normal message, but a recipient gene can respond to that message in an abnormal way. Thus creating another mutation. This mutation might take hundreds, thousands, hundreds of thousands of generations to emerge. The newly born creature, be it insect, mammal, whatever, is slightly different to its parents. It's a freak of nature. It has longer wings than its parents, or shorter legs, or more elaborate patterns on its wings.

'It's easy to think with evolution that this is all somehow

designed. But it doesn't really happen like that. The freak is just a freak, but the extra fin might prove to be very useful to an animal trying to escape a predator, or catch prey. Or it could be a disaster, fouling up movement maybe. If it's a success the animal is more likely to get more than its fair share of mates. The freak genes are passed on to more offspring and a new line is born.'

She turns over, away from him, 'So does this always produce a new species?'

'Maybe, over time. But individuals in the same species can develop different responses to the same situation. When insects are sprayed with pesticide, the death rate is never 100 per cent. Sometimes some of the survivors have some mutant gene that protects them from the pesticide. So when all the others in its species are dead, the mutant survivor eats the plants, and it becomes harder to kill off the pest with the same pesticide because the mutant gene is passed on to its offspring. But they would not necessarily be defined as a new species. This guy called Melander discovered this in Washington State in 1913, but no one really listened to him. They were too busy trying to create more powerful pesticides.'

She yawns, lazily, 'Wow.'

'Yeah.'

'So how does this relate to the moths and the bats?'

'Oh yeah, that's how I started all this. Well, you know that saying, "as blind as a bat"? Well, it's totally not true. Bats have eyes and pretty good eyesight. They can hunt using their eyes. But maybe sometime in the very distant past, on really dark nights, when the moon wasn't in the sky, their eyesight wasn't that effective. They went hungry. Perhaps bats had more predators back then. Anyway, somewhere along the way some mutant gene threw up some early version of sonar which would have developed over time, and the bat with this gene was able to hunt whatever the light. I mean, I'm simplifying here, the mutant gene may have occurred before a bat was properly a bat, or at the same time it became a flying mammal, or only when it was fully airborne. I don't know.'

'And this bat was better at killing insects, and got the girl because of it.'

'Something like that. A bat with sonar is more likely to survive and have a better chance of producing young that survive than those without.'

'And to counter this, moths have evolved to hear the sonar?'

'Yeah. A moth knows when a bat is heading towards it. It knows how close it is... When it has a chance to fly away and when it should just drop to the ground. Just as it knows it can scare off birds by making eye patterns on its wings, or disguising itself as a bird dropping, or a piece of bark, or creating some chemical response to being eaten by making itself taste bad.'

She turns back into him, moving upwards until her lips rest on his cheek.

He carries on, 'Ever heard of Henry Walter Bates?'

'No.'

'He was around at the same time as Charles Darwin. Bates was obsessed with moths and butterflies and spent years in the Amazonian jungle, collecting them and studying them. He suffered from parasites, yellow fever, malaria, dysentery, loneliness. He even adopted a native child and then lost her to some disease. When he came out of the jungle he brought with him a theory. He thought that butterflies and moths that taste good to predators learned through natural selection to disguise themselves as bad tasting species – by mimicking their colourings and patterns. They don't make themselves taste bad, they just make themselves look like they taste bad.'

'You like moths don't you?'

'They amaze me.'

They both fall silent for a moment.

'Didn't this all start with a question about extinction?' she asked.

He could hardly remember, 'Yes. It did, didn't it? What was it?'

'I think I remember something about an absorbing barrier.'

'Absorbing barrier? Right.'

He paused to rethink, then continued.

'Look at this system we've been talking about, if we can call it a system. It seems to balance things out. If you look at the fossil records of extinctions, they hardly ever happen when species have evolved together over millions of years. They form some natural balance. They rely on each other, or they know how to live together – or at least how to tactfully survive. There might be one or two background extinctions per million each year but nothing more. On a big scale, extinctions happen if there is some big event external to their day-to-day lives, like a meteorite impact or a volcanic explosion, or if there's a massive increase or decrease in temperature, or if two species that do not know how to live in balance are pushed together for some reason.'

'How do you know all this?'

'You get two layers of rock. One on top of the other. The layer underneath the rock is full of fossils from one period. The layer on top has fossils from another period. The top layer has fewer species than the one beneath. Sometimes the difference between the two layers of rock is defined by some big event.'

'Like KT, the thing that wiped out dinosaurs.'

'Yeah, the meteorite impact. Wham. No more dinosaur fossils. The end of an entire class of species.'

'But not a phylum?'

'No. You still get animals with backbones. But here's the scary part. Until man comes along the only major extinction records are from wipe-out scenarios. There's an extinction event and the higher layer of rock has 20 per cent less species, or 60 per cent, occasionally higher. But wherever *Homo sapiens* makes an appearance on a new continent, or an island somewhere, species just disappear. And this is ancient Man we're talking about, not modern Man, species just disappear from the fossil record. Australia, 46,000 years ago, then Europe 30,000 years ago, Eurasia 14,000 years ago. America. Everywhere, the most amazing species – horned tortoises as long as a car, sabre-toothed cats, mammoths, gigantic sloths. In Australia they lost 95 per cent of land animals weighing more than 45 kilos, in America 75 per cent. You can see it in the layers of rock. Now you see them, now you don't.

'And then, when the continents are cleared, humans move on to the islands. Hawaii! Before man turned up, the island had no mosquitoes, no ants, no stinging wasps, no venomous snakes or spiders. Now it has them all. The islands had 125 birds found nowhere else. Now there's only 35 left, 24 are endangered, a dozen or so, so rare they are beyond recovery. On Cyprus there were pygmy hippos and elephants just as high as your waist. On Crete, gigantic eagles. In Cuba huge flightless owls. The Polynesians ate their way through 2,000 species of birds. There are only 8,000 species living today. Imagine... one fifth of the species wiped out by one culture. And then, 500 years ago, Europeans sweep over the world again. This time they bring rats, pigs, agriculture, guns. And more extinctions. Humans are the X-factor for absorbing barriers throughout history. Humans blow evolution away, and all that's left for all these species is luck. If that goes, they go.

'I'll give you a modern example. There's a butterfly, called Schaus's Swallowtail, that's part of a captive breeding programme in a Florida university. It used to be numerous across Florida but then man chopped down its habitat and killed huge numbers with insecticide. Actually they were trying to kill mosquitoes, but the Swallowtail got in the way. "Collateral damage." So by 1992 there's only a few colonies left in a national park in Florida. But then Hurricane Andrew blows the whole place to smithereens and with it the Schaus's Swallowtail. If something happens to the university the final little buffer against extinction will be gone too.'

He pauses for a moment: 'I want to show you something in the book.'

He opens a section of the book with several drawings of flowers – a name by each one.

Filipendula ulmaria

Jasminum officianale

Digitalis purpurea f. albiflora

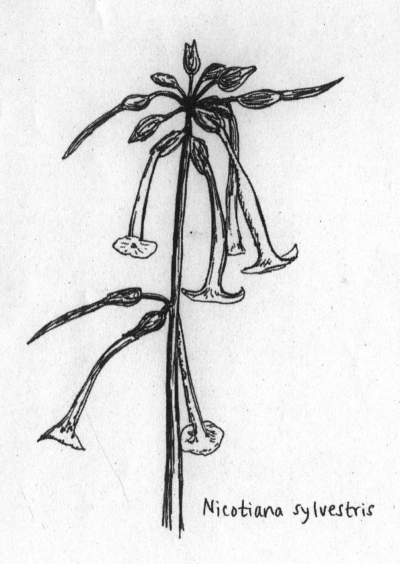

Nicotiana sylvestris

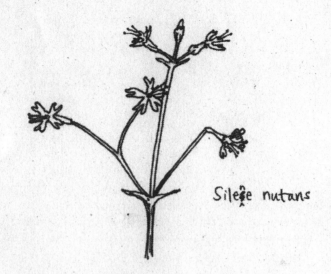

Silege nutans

Oenothera biennis

'All these plants are in the garden. I planted them because they open their flowers at night, or release a scent, or because they look good in the moonlight, or because they attract moths.'

'Why do people use all these Latin names?'

'I was just coming to that.'

'OK. Carry on.'

'The problem with common names is that they vary from country to country, or even between different parts of the same country. The Latin name standardizes things. Each plant name has two parts, the first part of the name lumps a plant in with its closest relatives. The genus. The second part identifies their individuality as a species.'

'This one's got three names.'

'The *Digitalis*; right. Well *Digitalis* is the genus name for foxgloves. *Purpurea* is a species of foxglove. The third name is a variety of the species *purpurea*, distinct from other varieties but part of the same species. *Albiflora* refers to the colours of its flowers, which are white. It's confusing at first, I know, but you get used to. Any plant with *albi*, *alba*, or *albus* in the name means white-flowered plant. *Sibirica* means it came from Siberia. Plants with *japonica* in the name come from Japan. Anyway, this classification system was invented by a Swedish guy called Linnaeus to allow scientists to talk to each other without getting confused about which species they were talking about. Once an official Latin name was chosen, there was no dispute.'

'So why Latin?'

'For one thing, it doesn't belong to any one country, but it also allowed the plant namers to be poetic with their names. They referenced the gods, women, human sexual organs.'

'Sounds like a typical boys' thing to do.'

'It was all a bit *Carry On* at times. Linnaeus compared plants to relationships, describing marriages, or concubines. He nicknamed his own wife a Monandrian lily – a virgin with a single husband. I don't really know why as they had kids. But anyway, I'm getting off the point. The point I was going to make was that Linnaeus was quite brilliant. He managed to classify species in a way that has allowed people to share information about plants and animals for two hundred years...'

'But...?'

'But... He had this grand scheme to turn his country into an economic powerhouse by introducing plants from all over the world to grow in Sweden. He thought he could fool warm loving plants to adapt to a cold climate by starting them off in the warmer southern parts of his country and moving them further north as the years went by.'

'It didn't work.'

'No. It just doesn't work like that. There are fossil records of the final part of the last ice age that show the rate at which the ice flow receded. It works out at about 120 miles a century. But the only trees that could fill the gap the ice flow left were a couple of species of spruce. They kept pace with the ice flow and formed huge forests across North America. Everything else could only extend its range by 25 miles every century. What Linnaeus thought of as slow adaptation, his slow, just wasn't slow enough. He pauses for a moment.

'Whatever people are thinking about global warming they aren't thinking enough.'

'Is that what's going to happen with global warming? I mean, things not being able to adapt quickly enough.'

'Pretty much. Plants and animals exist within certain temperatures zones. With global warming most temperature zones will move north, or south if you are in the southern hemisphere. Species have to follow their temperature zone to stay alive. But sometimes they can't do this, either because they are surrounded by ocean or mountains or some man-made obstacle like a city, or just because they rely on other species found only in that area. Does that make sense?'

'Kind of.'

'Let me think of an example. OK; two British butterflies. One, the silver studded blue butterfly, survives on lowland heath and can't move north because there are too many big gaps between heath to make the journey possible. The other, the comma butterfly, feeds on nettles and has moved 160 miles north in the last twenty years.'

'So the specialist species are more vulnerable?'

'Yes. In the short term. Conservationists have a real problem maintaining patches of habitat for species as it is, but if they can't predict where the species need to move to as the temperatures go up, its going to be really hard to make a place for them. In the long term, though, the problem goes beyond conservationists. We could be talking about as many as 37% of species disappearing. No one knows what this will mean for humans. Loss of food, medicine, culture, economic prosperity. We're tied more than we think.'

'Is this happening now?'

'The regions closer to the poles are warming up quickest first.'

He shows her another page from his Memory Book.

'Here, read this. I'm done talking.' He hands her the book and slides back down into the hammock, gently singing to the moon.

'Buffalo girls won't you come out tonight, come out tonight. Buffalo girls won't you come out tonight and dance by the light of the moon...'

She reads the page over.

Date: September 17th 2004

Notes from 'National Geographic', Sept 2004, on the effects of global warming on species loss.

Ecologist Bill Fraser has been studying Adelie penguins for thirty years — in that time the temperature has risen by 9 degrees Farenheit and the number of breeding pairs has dropped from 32,000 to 11,000. "The Adelies are the canaries in the coal mine of climate change in the Antarctic. Lesson number one for me has been the realization that ecology and eco-systems can change", he snaps his fingers, 'like that.' Fraser remembers an early encounter with the Adelies. He spotted a female, her breastbone ripped away by a seal. Fraser could look inside her wound to see her lungs. The Adelie hovered around her chicks, scarcely moving for a week while her mate foraged for food. Then, her wounds partly healed, she headed to sea and resumed feeding her offspring. "Adelies are the toughest animals

I've ever encountered. They can swim 3,500
miles in a winter migration. They thrive in
what has to be the hardest environment on
the planet. That's what angers me about
the whole picture, that these incredible
animals have to take it in the neck because a
bunch of humans can't get together to decide
what to do about the planet."

She rests the book on her lap and looks at the moth collector for a moment. His eyes are closed but she can see that he has been crying. The moisture around his eyes glistens in the moonlight. Not sure what to do or say, she carries on flicking through the memory book. On one page she finds a list.

Extinct animals, taken from 'A Gap in Nature'

- Upland Moa, 1500 – New Zealand
- Stellar's Sea Cow, 1768 – Commander Islands,
  Bering Sea
- Tahitian Sandpiper, 1777 – Tahiti
- White Gallinule, 1788 – Lord Howe Island,
  Australia

- Bluebuck, 1800 – South Africa
- Small Mauritian Flying Fox, 1800s – Mauritius
- Mysterious Starling, 1825 – Cook Islands
- Huppe, 1840 – Reunion Islands
- ~~Big Eared Bat~~
- Big Eared Hopping Mouse, 1843 – Australia
- Great Auk, 1844 – Hebrides and Iceland
- White Footed Rabbit-rat, 1845 – Australia
- Spectacled Cormorant, 1850 – Baring and
  Commander Island
- Norfolk Island Kaka, 1851 – Norfolk Island,
  Australia

- Falkland Islands Dog, 1876 – Falkland Islands
- Laughing Owl, 1914 – New Zealand
- Ilin Islands Cloudrunner, 1953 – Philippines

· Slender Bush Wren, 1972 – New Zealand
· Atitlan Grebe, 1989 – Guatemala

   Upland Moa, living on New Zealand for
thousands of years, within 300 years of man's
arrival it's gone. Stellar's Sea Cow, that was
unlucky. Kept away from humans, until some
sailors washed up on its island after their ship
was wrecked. 27 years later they're all gone.
Falkland Island Dog, so friendly they waded out
into the sea to greet landing parties. Hunters
used to hold a piece of meat to tempt them in one
hand and a knife to kill them in the other.
Great Auk. This is a classic. Eaten by explorers,
used as bait by fishermen, the last one on
St Kilda's was beaten to death by the islanders
because they thought it might be a witch.

On another, the names of extinct or endangered moths.

British moths – endangered and extinct

Netted carpet
Rosy Marsh Moth
Silurian
Conformist
Dotted Footman
Broad Bordered White Underwing
Pale Shining Brown
White Spot
Grey
Toadflax Brocade
Southern Chestnut
Heart Moth
White Spotted Pinion
Least Minor
Concolorous
Fenny Wainscot
Sandhill Rustic
Blair's Wainscot
Brighton Wainscot
Marsh Moth
Reddish Buff

Light & Dark Crimson
          Underwing
Scarce Blackneck
Bloxworth Snout
Shaded Fan Foot
Olive Crescent

Eventually she finds a block of pages made up of a single long essay typed on to seperate pages and stuck in the memory book. She reads it all.

I spent the night counting moths. I moved
between a number of traps set in a small
colosseum of light I had created with candles
placed in some glass jars around the garden. I
used wine rope traps hung from the bird cherry,
and watched the moths feed on them. I brought
out a white cotton bed-sheet and hung it on a
washing line strung between two trees. Above it
I fixed a bulb. I used the mercury vapour light
trap. While the sheet trap was slow to work, the
mercury vapour trap drew moths in quickly. I
watched how the moths reacted to the light. Most
moths just flew straight in to it. Others came
in, went away and then came back again. And some
didn't seem bothered by the light at all. Some
people say that moths fly to bright lights
because the moths imagine they have reached the
moon. I don't know if this is true. If it was,
they would spiral into the lights, as if they
were trying to keep the moon in the right place
in the sky in relation to ___ their flight,
endlessley self-correcting their flight path.
Most of the moths I watched last night didn't
spiral. The trap filled quickly though, and
every half an hour, or sometimes less, I took it
over to the shed and emptied the moths out into
the shed. I closed the shed door behind me,

turned off the light and opened the lid of the
trap. Low-level moonlight shone through the
window and as the moths emerged from the trap
into the greater space of the shed I closed my
eyes, and, holding the lightened trap in my arms
imagined I could feel the weight of freedom. Of
course, whatever lift I might have felt was just
an illusion, for you could fill the trap with a
hundred moths and the change in weight could
hardly be felt. When released they flew around
the shed with tremendous excitement. I guessed
they were mostly restless lovesick males brought
to flight by the scent of a female, only to be
seduced by the light of the mercury vapour trap.
I felt as though I had jailed them for the night
to cool off. I imagined tiny molecules of
pheromone scent pulsing through them, their
bodies overwhelmed by nerve impulses. Even after
a few minutes in the shed they must still know
where their mate is. And want to fly to her. But
life will go on without these trapped male
moths.
    Sometimes I worry that I have trapped some
moths that only live for a day like Acentria
ephemerella, the Water Veneer, and that I have
stolen their chance from them.
    As the night passed, and I made countless
journeys to the shed with my trap, the shed
filled up with moths. I thought I was getting
better at identifying some of the moths, but it
really is a long and sometimes tedious process.
I pore through the pages of the field guide to
get them in my head, but who can remember the
minute differences between a thousand types of
moth? Sometimes I think I am never going to be
good at this. But then I have a breakthrough and
the patterns on their wings start to make sense.

Some are easier than others. There is a moth with black, grey and white wing markings that's called a Setaceous 'Hebrew Character', because the markings at the front of its wings - a light blotch, with the two dark saddle shaped marks on either side - resemble a letter from the Hebrew alphabet. Each night I find something new. A new name to fall in love with. Canary Shouldered Thorn, Green Carpet, Common Carpet, Lilac Beauty, Scorched Wing, Buff Arches, Sallow Kitten, Puss Moth, Iron Prominent, Pebble Prominent, Lunar Marbled Brown, Flame Shoulder, Grey Dagger, Old Lady, Angle Shades, Frosted Orange, Burnished Brass, Silver Y, Spectacle. I think my favourite is Beautiful Golden Y. If I had to ask the most important question in the world it would be a beautiful golden y.

Last night I tried to identify them on the wing, and I know some people can, but I found it impossible. At three in the morning I switched the mercury vapour light off and stood amongst the moths I had already collected in the shed. The place was in uproar. A thousand moths flew around me. I closed my eyes and let them brush my hands and face. I could feel the presence of God, or creation, or evolution, or just the energy of time. As if it was contained in my shed. Trying to push out the walls and the door and the window. The wing beats were like African drums. Each moth, a separate note in a rhythmic, syncopated symphony of life, driven by sexual energy and longing. I was driven into the garden by their energy. But even here the energy was intense. The air was thick with life, highways of flight stacked one above the other. Cross-town traffic. Lit by the moon. The wind-rushed

reeds by the pond quavered the air with shrill
notes. Boughs of tree leaves rose and fell in
small time frenzies. The breeze threw ripples
across the pond. Frogs watched them. The water
lilies rose above the surface of the water like
white witches of Atlantis, held afloat on great
rafts of leaves, seducing me into a
vacuum of timelessness. Each one of them with
stamens so flushed with gold they glowed. I
couldn't take my eyes off them. I brushed the
leaves of the watermint. And inhaled peppermint.
I hoped to see a Water Veneer emerge from its
underwater chrysalis. None did. Instead I
watched a half submerged whip tongued frog
making the most of whatever came its way. The
white sunflowers by the shed looked like dwarfed
angels in the moonlight. Five halos floating in
air. A slug moved sickeningly up one stalk. A
group of ants up another. In Panama ants protect
caterpillars. In Wales they eat them. I pity any
chrysalis buried under the glutinous soil.
     I watched the ivy for a while by torchlight.
Out of the way of the flight paths of moths this
is a world full of quiet purposeful energy,
where the only sound you can hear is the faint
crack of ivy stems as they move under the weight
of a passing snail or slug. In this habitat of
ivy leaves I can watch the slugs eating with
interest rather than some giddy queasiness. Now
I know why the ivy has to grow so fast. All the
garden grazers congregate here, agitating it
into growth. The snails move like tug boats,
slow but with great power and purpose. In the
daytime, woodlice look like poor timid little
creatures, scuttling away from us under rocks
and wood. Despite their armoury they are bullied

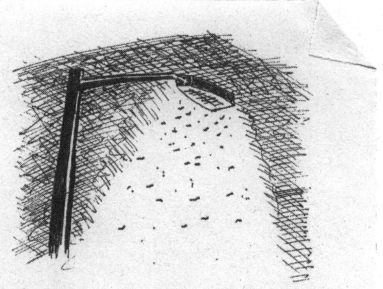

by the sun. But last night I watched one defy an
Everest-like drop to reach the end of a
~~~~~~~~~~~ precipitous thread of ivy. It did
not seem burdened by weight or gravity. There
were ants around, but not in groups. They worked
individually, one looking over a flower, another
tapping a leaf, for what reason I cannot say.
Only the spiders were still. All except one
woodlouse spider I found hunting. From my
elevated position I could see the top of the
streetlight. I watched the arc of orange light
descending from it towards the road beneath.
There must have been a moth inhabiting every
square centimetre. Each one a fluorescent spark
of orange light. They bounced off the lamp like
balls of water off a hotplate. Now and then a
large moth shot up from the ground like a
firecracker, and danced like Tinkerbell in the
light before sweeping out of the arc of light or
back to the floor again. Some looked as big as

birds. Bats swung in and out of the light like a
pendulum. Each swing deadly. After half an hour
I brought my eyes down from this
trapezing moth circus of light and stared
blissfully at the flowers of the white poppies,
which lay open and familiar. Each one a
celestial invitation.

   I left the moths alone in the shed until they
were quietened by the light of dawn through the
shed window, and went back in to count them. It
was past four in the morning. I had gone beyond
the barrier of the desire to sleep, and entered
an almost euphoric state of alertness. This time
of day is like no other. When I have been awake
all night, like this, I like nothing better than
to talk. The conversation is always out of the
ordinary, as if the process of staying awake has
changed us. To be alone at this time with
nothing to do and no one to talk to is scant
reward for the effort of being up. I remembered
the night I found a garden at Glastonbury
Festival.

   I had spent much of the night wandering
through the busy parts, where the colours and
the lights are big and explosive, where it feels
sometimes like day. Where vast numbers of people
march through the illumination from one
amusement to another, their faces harshly lit.
And the trees are all visible from root to
crown. In these parts you can see how
destructive light can be, for the mystery of
darkness is vanquished by electricity.
Everything is obvious. The bright colours of
day, the painted faces, the ballroom gowns some
people wear. The late night tired energy of
crowds. All the people looking for some
indefinable experience. Expectant faces and

tired feet marching inharmoniously. The mind
driving on the body without consideration. There
is nothing to suggest in this light that there
are any secrets in the world. The world is all
laid out in front of you.

   After a while I grew tired of this carnival
and drew myself away to the quieter parts of the
festival. Here the paths were lit by flame; oil
lamps in exotic metal cages; candles in old tin
cans punctured with a hundred holes,
or in painted jamjars; flares pushed into the
ground in curved patterns. In one place I came
across an expanse of white paper bags, each one
lit from inside by a small tea light placed on
top of a handful of sand or earth to stop the
paper catching. In the middle of these springs
of light a man played guitar and a couple danced
closely together. The guitarist watched the
movement of the couples feet as he played. You
could see clearly the hem of her frock and the
colour of his boots, which were red. The rest of
the contours of their bodies were hardly
visible. Apart from their faces. For although
their faces were partly buried in each others
shoulders you could still see the creases of
their smiles as they turned into the light. One
after the other, light and darkness. Their
faces, drooping over one another like two

wilting sunflowers, orbiting each other as if
they were planets in their own universe. No
space around them. In my mind's eye I could see
the sunflower heads in my garden lit with this
quiet light. You would only see a small part of
their reality. But it would be enough to fuel
something in the imagination. Whatever
inspiration you chose to take from a living
thing. I watched the couple for some time and
then moved beyond them, moving quietly through
the spaces between the paper bags until I left
that whole space and entered another, a garden
made for the night.

The garden was lit in part by fairy lights
strung from a grand old oak tree, whose crown
sheltered a seating area backed by a curved wall
of planked wood. The lights were strung high
enough to keep the fat of the light with the
tree. And the seating area unsaturated. Away
from this, candles gave out a skinny glow. The
garden created moments of quiet intimacy for
those who spent even just a short time in it.
Contained gladly in this ⸻ harmonious
setting of natural forms, people huddled into
pairs, and into groups of threes or fours. Their
conversation coalesced into a rich, generous
hum. Soft and energetic.

The garden was a collection of small flower-
beds raised out of the Glastonbury soil with
rough shawn wooden edging, cut in thin wedges
from the milled carcasses of great timbers, and
filled with compost and various aromatic herbs.
In amongst the herbs I could clearly see the
whites of oxeye daisy flowers and of wild
strawberries, raised in clusters of six or seven
above their own dark foliage.

These flower-beds were surrounded by a circle

of organic wooden structures, each with its own
personality - not so much plain clothed, as
without uniform. One was shaped like the upturned hull of a boat and roofed with hundreds
of individually cut wooden tiles. Another was a
large hollow onion made from finely woven wands
of willow - into which two or three people could
squeeze if they folded their bodies into the
curves of the structure. A third was simply a
canvas slung over bent rods of hazel pushed into
the ground and tied together with rope. The
space within each structure was different to the
one next to it and each related to the night in
a different way - creating a different set of
expectations and illusions for those that
occupied them.

The canvas created a deep darkness under it,
and those that lay there talked very quietly
indeed, or not at all. Some only slept. This was
a place to go when the night had become too much
and the body longed for day. The boat structure
was more open to the night, and light crept into
it, even to the deepest point of the hull. Even
so there was more shadow than light, and what
light there was illuminated the lowest things -
blades of grass, ankles, hands palmed down on
rugs, cushions, the flaps of trouser legs.
Inside this structure the people sat. They did
not lie. They talked. I imagined that some were
pairs just met, not yet coupled. Finding out all
they could about each other with an intimacy
that was as natural as the wood that surrounded
them. This was a safe place to forge friendship.
Calm, private and real.

Inside the onion a different game could be
played out. This was a childhood den for adults.
Here there was laughter, and the laughter was as
bright as sunlight. Despite the lateness of the
hour the faces of the inhabitants, which were
clearly lit, were still fresh with energy.
In the centre of the garden a net had been
strung between several large wooden stakes,
pinched into the ground. The net was strong
enough for several people to lie around in it
and I climbed aboard, smiling at the people who
were already there. Not really listening to
their conversation, I lay back into the net and
looked up at the sky. Someone had covered a
small glass jam jar with layers of coloured
tissue paper, placed a candle inside it and hung
it over the middle of the net. The light that
shone through was diffused through greens, blues
and reds. It shone not only downwards but to the
sides and upwards. It illuminated the arched tip
of the length of hazel that supported it. Beyond
the candle, at a slight angle away from it to
the east hung the moon. When I lay back in the
net and looked up at them both I could almost
imagine I lived on a planet with two moons.
I started listening to the conversation of the
strangers in the net. One of them told a story
of creation I had never heard before. The story
of the first night on earth, at least how it was
imagined by the ____ Maoris. About their two
gods, one each representing the earth and the
sky. And how there was no light. Only darkness.
And how between them these two gods had seventy
children. But because the sky and the earth were
so close together there wasn't room for seventy
children. So the children climbed on one
anothers shoulders and pushed the sky away from

the earth. And for the first time light reached
the earth. And night followed day.

It struck me that in essence this explanation
was the same as the Christian belief, or for
that matter the scientific explanation of
creation - that light was created out of
darkness. That the night came first. Moths came
before butterflies.

I looked up at the two moons above me and
raised my feet up to them, which made the person
next to me laugh and do the same. And so it
continued until there were twelve feet in the
air - all paddling round one another and falling
over each other and pushing up at the moons,
until we were all giddy with laughter and dizzy
from being upside down.

After that I visited the garden and the net on
several nights. When I was there alone I lay in
the centre, looking up at the stars, thinking
about my garden at home. It allowed me to make a
connection. It was a spot of plain familiarity
in a shower storm of luminescence. When I was
there with friends we would fill up the net. We
would lie close to each other, talking in a way
we rarely had time for through the rest of the
busy fragmented year. I carry these moments like
a lantern through the harsh quiet nights of
winter. A glow worm memory of tenderness. If my
world ends with a love like this I should have
no cause to complain.

Last night I had no one to talk to. These
nights can be good too. When I count moths I
feel as calm and as still as they are. As if I

too am hiding from the reality of light. I
cannot haven myself more snugly in a harbour of
peace and tranquillity than when I walk around
my shed in an early morning. I could not hold a
hundred different species of bird in my shed, or
the mammals of the African plains, or the great
whales of the oceans. I would not want a hundred
snakes. A hundred frogs would make too much
noise. A hundred beetles would scuttle me into
irritation. But a hundred species of resting
moths, made tired by the day, fills me with calm
wonder. Tiffany's holds fewer jewels. Emeralds,
rubies, golds, the whites of diamonds and
pearls. This is my cure for the mean reds. And
those moths that choose to wear browns or greens
or blacks do so with an infinite variety of
patterns and colour . pigments. All
around I am caught in the glare of phoney eyed
wings. Some moths try to hide themselves against
the wooden panels of the shed, but there is yet
to have evolved a moth that looks like it has
been bought from a hardware store. Only the
Spectacle moth carries the look of something
made by man.

One by one I count them all, each time making
a note in my book. It's a wondrous thing to be
the only species capable of creating a logical
scientific method for recording the passing of
another species. To divide the world into 10km
squares and count what we find there is a
strange gift. Of course I looked for an Orange
Upperwing without success. When the counting was
done I left the shed and closed the door behind

me. I shall open it again tomorrow night and let them all out. On the way down to the house I noticed that the flowers of the Nottingham Catchfly had closed for the day. I shall go` and watch them open again at seven.

She feels like he has created a fragile beautiful world for himself, but wonders whether it is all as real as he supposes. She finds the Orange Upperwing's page and reads it over.

Orange Upperwing (Jodia croceago)

Used to be common. Historical distribution included Wiltshire, Oxfordshire, the West Midlands and the Isle of Wight. Recorded in fair numbers on the border of Surrey and West Sussex up until 1977 but last seen there in 1983. Also seen in Cornwall (1983), East Sussex (1984), North Hampshire (1992).

- Singletons seen in Aber Magwyr in 1955 and Llechryd in 1982.

- Last confirmed sighting – six individuals between 5th October and 4th November 1994 between Cardigan and Aberystwyth!

It reads like a crime report. 'Last seen.' 'Last confirmed sighting.' She imagines Nick Ross on Crimewatch. 'Don't have nightmares. Species don't disappear every day.' And then she thinks that maybe they do, and she just doesn't know about it.

She can't bear the silence any longer.

'What's a singleton?' She asks the moth collector, quickly.

'What? Oh, it's just the name we use to describe a moth seen on its own.'

'It's a lonely word isn't it. I'm glad we're not singletons.'

'Do you know what they call the last living example of a species?'

'Is this going to make *me* cry?'

'Endling.'

7

Alone, on the northern edge of his lawn, the moth collector will sometimes succumb to the fragrance of wild garlic[10] or sweet rocket[11] and lie close by with a jumper pillowing his head on the dew damp ground. From here he will look up at the peeled back petals of the 24 hour flower of a white day lily[12], which, trying to make the most of its one day on Earth, looks to him like the mouth of a trumpet blown out by its own exuberance. And he will gaze at the long summer blooms of the bell towered foxgloves. Sometimes he looks at the cabled towers of flower bells, and exploded trumpets, through the lense of a camera and brings the moon behind in and out of focus. Trumpets, bells and moon. Trumpets, bells and moon.

And then, still lying on his back, he moves the lens around in a slow circular sweep, just to see what he can see. Through the viewfinder he will catch the blurred shimmer of a spider's web, strung between apple branches like a lace doily, and focus the lens pin sharp onto its inhabitant.

Once, from this position, he had watched an Eyed Hawkmoth[13] (so called because the pigments on the scales of its wings make a pattern that birds mistake for the eyes of a predator) crash into the lair of a walnut spider[14]. When it happened the moth collector sat up quickly, turned around to face the orbed web and pushed the camera lens close in to the moth. Blue ringed black pupils blinked at him as the moth hinged its wings open and shut. It's deep bloodshot iris pointing downwards with the sad indiscretion of a lost drunk.

The silk threads of the web vibrated like plucked guitar strings, and the walnut spider clung to them like a note in the air. Afraid of flightlessness, the Eyed Hawkmoth thrashed in this bed of silk like a child wrestling with nightmares, pulling at threads, tossing this way and that, closing the web around itself, doing the spider's job for it.

The moth collector had wondered whether to intervene. A god of Rome sent down from the heavens to save a mortal warrior with a quick poke of a finger. But it wasn't his way, and he watched instead with the detached consciousness of a war zone photographer, albeit a giant one.

In the end the outcome had been neutral. Fearing the destruction of its web, or perhaps mistaking it for something more dangerous, the spider cut the threads around the Hawkmoth and it fell to the ground in a duvet of silk threads, to continue its struggle at ground level, lest it be snaffled by some opportunistic rodent. The spider rebuilt its web, pushing silk threads through spinnerets on its abdomen, each one as clean and strong as a freshly rolled steel rod.

The moth collector can be as patient as a spider when he wants to be. Waiting for something to happen is almost a hobby for him. He could list it on customer surveys, safe in the knowledge that he would never get a single piece of junk mail about it through the letterbox. What can be sold to a man who is satisfied by the pleasure of waiting?

Once he spent an hour watching two crab spiders mate[15]. It happened one evening, as a sunset reddened the sky. He sat on a rough cut log by the lip of a bed full of sweet-smelling Nottingham Catchfly at the southern edge of his garden, looking out over the idle chimney pots of his terrace to the Welsh grassland savannah that folded out beyond. An open flood plain of sheep, willow and hazel, split in two by a river and quartered by a railway line.

He was thinking about sunsets and chimpanzees. Trying to work out whether he appreciated a sunset more, or less, now that he knew the scientific explanation for it, or whether it mattered at all. Chimpanzees can appreciate a good sunset without thinking, 'Ooh, I do like it when those air molecules block out the blues and violets in light. I'm so glad that light has to pass through 38 times more atmosphere to reach us at this time of day.' They just go to the edge of a forest and watch.

But then the ghostly pale lemon wings of a Swallowtailed moth[16], attracted no doubt by the scent of the Nottingham Catchfly by his side, passed before his eyes and drew his gaze down to the flowers' little white petals. And there he saw them, beneath the flowers on a small grey stone, two brown crab spiders engaged in a courtship. One on top of the other. The top one circled over the body of the one beneath, back and forth and side to side. When the moth collector took in the scene properly, he realised that the bottommost spider was being tied down to the stone with silk – an act of high class bondage which, once complete, allowed the one on top, who he guessed to be the male, rightly as it turned out when he looked it up in a book later, to get on with the business of mating.

Imagining the whole deal to be over in a matter of minutes, he was suprised to find himself still peering at the pair an hour later, when, in the fading half light of dusk, the sunset long gone, the male spider finally walked away, leaving the female to untangle herself from the silk and go about her business.

When he finally looked up the moth collector was conscious that time had moved on.

8

He watched the day pushed aside by the night, a line of darkness crossing the sky. He could see why meteorologists call it the terminator line. He took out a couple of large thick candles from a metal tin brought up from the house, lit them both and placed them on the edge of the wall. It was one of those rare nights where the air, with no place to go, stills itself to apathetic tranquility. If the candles flicker, they have only themselves to blame.

A few moths circled the lights. The moth collector took a small hardback notebook from his trouser pocket and made a record of each of the new arrivals in neat handwriting. Buff Tip, Vapourer, Rosy Footman, Garden Tiger[17]. All moths he had seen before.

It was difficult to keep a neat hand in the darkness so he walked over to the shed to turn a light on. Finding the door ajar, he slipped his hand through the gap and flicked a switch inside. He withdrew his hand when the bulb lit up, closed the door and moved round to the front of the shed, where light poured out through a small dusty window. He stood by the window and made notes in his book.

July 2nd 2005, calm, airless, dry, 10.05pm

Buff Tip - three
Vapourer - singleton
Rosy Footman - singleton
Garden Tiger - two

The harsh light of the bulb cast a pool of brightness over the front of the garden. He watched evening primrose[18] flowers caught up in the glare: new yellow cups fresh from the potter's oven, fragile and warm.

A Heart And Dart[19] beat against the window pane, its dark brown wings treading air. The moth collector noted the new sighting in his book.

He looked beyond the moth, through the dusted glass, to the scene of cleanliness and order he had created inside the shed.

Just beyond the glass a large, shallow crate squatted broad and deep on a rough wooden table. A decade of Welsh sunlight had barely faded the inked lettering on the side of the crate. It was still possible to tell that once it had been the property of a Cypriot tomato grower. Inside the crate, a leprechaun's causeway of hexagonal glass jars pressed up against each other. To the left of it a notebook lay open on a desk; two pens resting in a serene cleavage of paper. A pile of books filled a space the other side of the crate. On the wall behind, a set of shelves carried the weight of a miscellaneous assortment of old biscuit tins, and the paraphernalia of the moth collector's passion. A small, boxed telescope, various unopened boxes of candles, a mercury vapour moth trap. Everything in its place. The mercury vapour trap looked like a topsy-turvy table lamp, the kind Alice might find through the looking glass, with the shade on the bottom and a light bulb poking out of a small hole in the top.

The moth collector grew tired of the light. He moved round to the side of the shed, opened the door and stepped inside. Two or three moths were now beating at the window. He found the noise oppressive. Opening one of the biscuit tins he brought out a couple of large thick candles and placed them on the desk. Lifting a box of matches from his pocket he struck one against the rough edge of a shelf and held the flame against the wick of a candle, and then against the one next to it. He turned the light off and felt a weight lift as the moths fell away from the window. He closed the door behind him and sat down. He opened up his Memory Book and flicked through a few pages. Feeling slightly drowsy, he placed his arms on the desk and rested his head on top of them. And drifted...

9

The moth collector is ready to dream at will. The scene could be set on midsummer night or Christmas Eve, or any of many nights in between. The dreams are often the same. And the position of his hunched body. This Christmas Eve, with his gloved hands resting on his Memory Book, and his little paraffin stove drawn in tight, the moth collector's drowsy mind crashes into old nights gone like a drunken elephant let loose in an Indian bazaar. Recollections tumble under foot as the elephant moves from stall to stall. Memories, dreams, imagined worlds, and the words in his Memory Book, all brought to cinematic life on his closed eye lids.

In one reel he counts out nineteen candles and places one each in nineteen hexagonal glass jars.

In another he sees shadows lean against plants.

In a third he holds a friend's outstretched hand near his chest and guides her through his garden blindfold. He lets her swallow the night sound blind, the beating of small wings, the shaking of leaves, the rattle of the air as it pushes around and through and up and down and over and between, forever channelling itself, unable in the restless night of his memory to stay seated in some calm nook of the garden. He watches the squinting frame of her eyelids press heavily against the cloth of her blindfold, straining at the material, her eyes unable to relax into their sockets.

In another reel he pictures in the great open landscape of his mind the pickers of pupae, the collectors of caterpillars, the inquistive hunters of lepidoptera, those who have staked with their collectors' board pins a small piece of history. Laying down in their ledgers the minute details of the discipline of their lives. Their passion logged in legs, and wings, antennae and abdomen. Proboscis and the patterns of colours laid against the backs of scales.

He sees a worn-robed woman meander towards madness along

Elizabethan hedgerows, poking the same with a stick to catch caterpillars in a cloth. This when the hedgerows of England were something; laid thick with life and ripe for exploration. It is Eleanor Glanville he sees, a woman of means, finding solitude away from her violent husband. A woman who paid the poor sixpence each for fine caterpillars, but died declared insane in a battle for her fortune because she dressed like a gypsy and searched the hedgerows for moths.

He sees a rich man, a sleeping, snoring rich man. A rich man whose limbs fall over the side of a bed which is too small for him. Through his own dreams the moth collector sees the dreams of this man. Walter Rothschild, one of the richest men in England, advisor to parliamentarians and kings, dreaming the same dreams he had dreamt since he was a child, in the same bed he had slept in since he was a child, of the two million moths and butterflies he had paid someone to collect since he was a child. If the moth collector sees him twitch in his bed, if he sees him wrestless. If he sees him haul his drooping limbs from one side of the bed to another, he wonders if he is perhaps thinking of the words of his Australian collector A.S. Meek, who, having caused the death of a native boy helper, wrote in his diary: "'I suppose that the people of the civilized countries will wonder that there was any doubt for a single moment in my mind as to whether the lives of the boys should be sacrificed for the sake of butterflies. But one gets not what I would call a recklessness or an indifference to human life so much as a different idea of its value"'.

Sometimes he will dive into the lakes of his imagination and come up breathless from the leap. As if he has surfaced from some deep Welsh pool where the water is pure, cold and ancient. On the surface of his imagined lake he will suck in the air, bob on the water and watch the infinite jigsaw of the night come together, assembled not by some unseen hand, but by the pieces themselves. He considers it an amazing feat that evolution has delivered a species so complex it can understand how simply it began. Of all those gifts bestowed upon humanity, comprehension and imagination are the greatest. A nightjar opens its gaping mouth to gather in moths as it flys. A bat sweeps low over the water and claps for its prey, bringing its wings in front of its body through a sweeping arc to collect a moth and bring it up to its mouth. An owl glides into the open gallery of the moth collector's mind and steals a great victory for itself. Pinching the wings of the bat inside its claws it passes out of frame and away over the shore where moths unfurl their tongues to draw up nectar from the flowers of bankside plants. As they move from flower to flower they carry pollens with them. In his imagination he can place the rainforest plant *Angraecum sesquipedale* on the shores of his Welsh pool and watch as the only living thing capable of reaching inside and propogating its prodigiously long flower (a moth by the way) arrives to do its job. To the moth collector the moth is the centre of the nocturnal world. Hardly a moment on this earth passes when a moth, or its egg, caterpillar or pupae is not being eaten by some passing bird, mammal, amphibian or insect. Nor a second when one has not brought into the world a new seed.

If, in his semi-conscious state he sometimes hears the rain against the roof, or the window, or the door with its old iron latch and hinges, or hears the air roll up the valley from the sea in a thunderous storm ball to rattle the lose screws in his shed, his mind thinks not of his own safety but that of wind blown, hair-raised, arched-backed caterpillars. In his mind they are hurrying off from picnics at the wurlizter edges of vibrating leaves as fast as their six legs can carry them, less they be flipped off like so many pancakes from a frying pan. Propelled downwards to bounce stickily in a hammock web, just enough to vibrate a spider into mindfulness, but not enough to bounce out again; or if they should luckily miss the web, to descend further down to earth where the ants and the shrews lie in wait. Or he thinks of battle hardened adult moths flying into explosive bombardments of rain drops, to them the size of puddles, or cannon-ball hail, and in his mind watches them beaten down towards the ground and into puddles the size of lakes where they suffocate in the clinging film of the surface of the water. If only they could muster the strength to pull their wings through the water. If they could do that, their bodies would surely follow. But they can't. They have fallen through a trap door which opens only one way. So tightly held is the water above them that it is as if it has been staked to the ground with rods of lightning. And, if a storm rages, he wonders, how many branches have snapped? How many trees will come down? How many creatures must find themselves a new home? And what would it be like living in this realm of hyperactivity? Of sudden relocation? What would it be like to be a refugee in this scuttling world of chaos, searching for a safe haven in the scuffed-up muddy earth with its puddles and predators? He consoles himself with the knowledge that insects only see what there is to do and not the possibility of what there is to come.

With such a thought in his mind this Christmas Eve he jolts awake, as if the elephant of his dreams has lifted him out of the busy market place and deposited him without a by or leave in a cold empty plane of wakefulness. Water from an upturned bottle drips on to an old tin box on the floor besides the table. The storm was an illusion. Christmas Eve is just as still as it was. But now the moth collector is not alone. Through clouded eyes he sees a little boy standing in the open doorway of his shed. Wrapped up in a gold dressing gown, drowned in moonlight, tender and loved, this little Welsh prince asks the question on any young child's lips at this time of year.

'Have you seen Father Christmas?'

Most children are content to stay in their rooms to look for Father Christmas. To twitch the curtains of their windows and press their noses up against the window pane, steaming that part up with their breath and drawing back to rub away the excited condensation with damp sleeves. But not all children have a granny with a Welsh hillside for a garden. With trees and a view. And a way of catching Father Christmas by surprise. And not all children can pull themselves up through their grandad's rooftop window and slide down slates to the garden. But this one can, and does; when no one is looking. And here he stands at the threshold of the moth collector's shed, looking brightly into the shadows of the shed, where the moth collector sits surrounded by flickers and wisps.

The little boy whispers, 'He has a present for me I think.'

'Yes I imagine he has,' the moth collector says.

Conscious of the cold air the boy is letting into the shed the moth collector invites him to sit and watch for Father Christmas through the window of the shed. Rooted firmly to the threshold of the shed the little boy scans the inside. He is looking for comfirmation of something. Unable to find it he decides instead to ask his question direct.

'Are you the moth collector?'

'The moth collector?'

'My nana told me the moth collector lived here.'

'Ahh. Well your nana is partly right. Only I don't collect moths. I never keep them. I just count them and let them go again.'

'Why do you count them?' The boy shivers a little and moves half a step closer to the heat of the stove.

'So I know if we are running out.' The moth collector takes two large pieces of cloth, picks up the fire with the cloths in his hands and moves the fire closer to the boy.

'Will we run out of moths?' The little boy asks.

'We might one day.' The moth collector replies.

'If we do, I will ask Father Christmas for some more for you.'

It is a solemn promise and the moth collector replies, 'OK,' with equal seriousness.

'Jake!' A third voice. The little boy's mother calls for him. 'Jake!'.

Her voice is familiar to the moth collector. It has a familial resemblance.

'If I'm not mistaken,' he says to the little boy, with a smile. 'That must be your mother. I think you should call her.'

'Mum. I've found the moth collector! I've found the moth collector!'

Following the sound of her son's voice, Jake's mother pushes open the little gate that divides the moth collector's garden from that of her parents and climbs the steps to reclaim her son.

'Mum, I looked for Father Christmas and I found the moth collector instead, only he doesn't collect moths, he just counts them. In case we run out.' He turns to the moth collector. 'That's right isn't it?'

'That's right,' the moth collector answers.

Jake's mother holds her son close to her and speaks to the moth collector. 'Maybe you should come and see this moth in Mum's garden.'

'Sure. What does it look like?'

'I saw it just now as I came through the gate. It's orange I think'.

The End

Extracts from the moth collector's

Memory Book

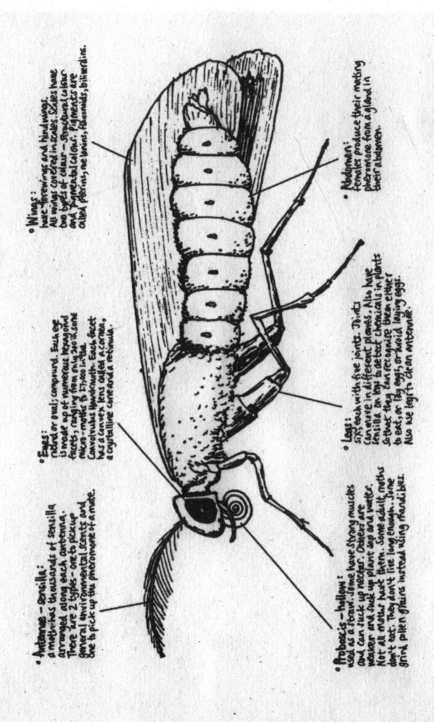

• Wings:
have forewings and hindwings. All wings covered in scales. Scales have two types of colour — Structural colour and Pigmental colour. Pigments are called pterins, melanins, flavonoids, biliverdins.

• Abdomen:
Females produce their mating pheromone from a gland in their abdomen.

• Eyes:
round or oval; compound. Each eye is made up of numerous hexagonal facets, ranging from only 200 in some micro-moths to 17,000 in the Convolvulus Hawkmoth. Each facet has a convex lens called a cornea, a crystalline cone and a retinula.

• Legs:
six, each with five joints. Joints can move in different planes. Also have sensilla on legs to detect chemicals in plants so that they can recognise them either to eat, or lay eggs, or avoid laying eggs. Also use legs to clean antennae.

• Antennae — sensilla:
a moth has thousands of sensilla arranged along each antenna. There are 2 types — one to pick up general environmental scents and one to pick up the pheromone of a mate.

• Proboscis — hollow:
used as a straw. Some have strong muscles and can suck up nectar. Others are weaker and suck up plant sap and water. Not all adult moths have them. Some adult moths don't eat. They don't live long enough. Some grind pollen grains instead using mandibles.

Life cycle of the Cinnabar Moth

Pupa hibernates on ground

Adult moth lays eggs on Ragwort
(Senecio jacobaea)
Caterpillars live and feed on Ragwort
Pupa hibernates on ground in loose
Cocoon among spun up leaves
Moths fly from May ti ll July,
late afternoon and dusk

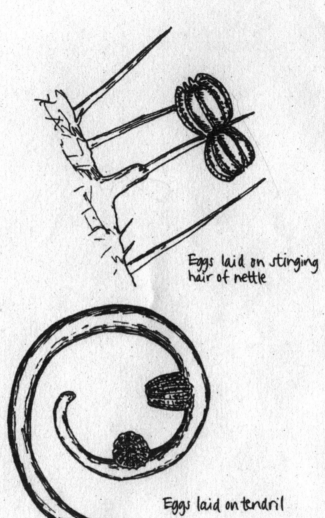

Eggs laid on stinging
hair of nettle

Eggs laid on tendril

Gardening for moths

Keep the garden sheltered. Use only native trees.
My old hedge fine.
- Silver birch - Betula pendula
    250 species of insect can live in a silver birch
- Goat willow - Salix caprea
- Elder - Sambucus nigra
- Oak - Quercus robur or (more native to Wales)
    Quercus petraea
- Rowan - Sorbus aucupari
- Hazel - Corylus avellana
- Beech - Fagus sylvatica

Use older varieties of plants that have flowers
with simple structures. Modern bred plants, such
as those with double blooms, often have reduced
levels of nectar. Cottage garden varieties are
good. Put plants in rows or drifts so that the
scent is easy to detect. Moths may find individual
specimens harder to find. Provide high nectar
plants and plant for a long season
of flowers. Nectar production can vary

depending on soil type, weather conditions and aspect. Keep sheltered!

Keep an area of long grass, a nettle patch and some log piles around the place for beetles. No pesticides! Leave plants to go to seed — many insects over-winter in them. Avoid winter tidying of the soil. Moth pupae and other over-wintering insects are disturbed by it.

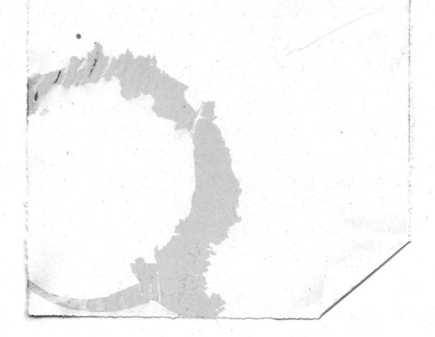

Evening Primrose

Plants that attract moths

- Achillea millefolium - Yarrow
- Allium schoenoprasum - Chives
- Aquilegia - Columbine
- Berberis vulgaris - Barberry
- Borago officinalis - Borage
- Calamintha clinopodium - Wild Basil
- Campanula rotundifolia - Harebell
- Ceanothus - Californian lilac
- Centaurea - Knapweed
- Centaurea nigra - Hardhead/Lesser Knapweed
- Centranthus ruber - Red Valerian
- Chrysanthemum leucanthemum - Ox-eye daisy
- Crambe maritima - Sea Kale
- Cynara cardunculus - Globe Artichoke
- Dianthus deltoids - Maiden Pink
- Digitalis purpurea - Common Foxglove
- Echium vulgare - Viper's bugloss
- Eryngium giganteum - 'Silver Ghost'
- Filipendula ulmaria - Meadowsweet
- Galium verum - Lady's Bedstraw
- Geum urbanum - Herb Bennet

- Geranium robertianum - Herb Robert
- Hebe - 'Great Orme'
- Helianthemum mummularium - Rock Rose
- Hesperis matronalis - Dame's Violet / Sweet Rocket
- Jasminum officianale - Common Jasmine
- Lavandula - Lavendar
- Linaria purpurea - Toadflax
- Lobelia cardinalis - Cardinal Flower
- Lonicera japonica - Honeysuckle
- Lythrum salicaria - Purple Loosestrife
- Marjoram hortensis - Majoram
- Melissa officinalis - Lemon Balm
- Mentha aquatica - Watermint
- Matthiola longipetula - Night Scented Stock
- Nicotiana sylvestris - Tobacco Plant
- Oenothera - Evening Primrose
- Origanum vulgare - Wild Marjoram
- Parthenocissus - Virginia Creeper
- Primula veris - Cowslip
- Primula vulgaris - Primrose
- Reseda luteola - Ragged Robin
- Rhamnus frangula - Alder Blackthorn

- Salix caprea - Sallow
- Salvia haematodes - Meadow Clary
- Salvia pratensis - Meadow Clary
- Saponaria officinalis - Soapwort
- Silene alba - White Campion
- Solidago candensis - Golden Rod
- Stachys germanica - Hedge Woundwort
- Stellaria holostea - Greater Stitchwort
- Trifolium pratense - Red Clover
- Verbascum - Mullein
- Verbena bonariensis - holds Royal Horticultural
       Society Award of Garden Merit (AGM)
- Viola tricolor - Field Pansy

Note: White Campion has two Latin names
    (must be varieties), as does Meadow Clary

Seasonal variations of nectar plants
attractive to butterflies and moths
- The Wildlife Trusts/RHS

Early season
· Aubretia
· Hyacinthoides non-scripta - English Bluebell
· Ribes sanguineum - Flowering Currant
· Muscari botryoides - Grape Hyacinth
· Pulmonaria spp - Lungwort
· ~~Prim~~ Primula vulgaris - Primrose
· Viola odorata - Sweet Violet
· Eranthis hyemalis - Winter Aconite
· Anemone nemerosa - Wood Anemone
· Alyssum saxitile - Yellow Alyssum

Mid season
· Buddleja davidii - Buddleia
· Calluna vulgaris - Heather
· Gallium verum - Lady's Bedstraw
· Lavendula spp - Lavendar
· Lavatera spp - Mallow
· Linaria purpurea - Purple Toadflax

- Arabis caucasica - Rock Cress
- Eryngium maritimum - Sea Holly
- Verbena bonariensis - Verbena
- Erysimum cheiri - Wallflower

Late season
- Echninacea purpurea - Coneflower
- Tagetes spp - French Marigold
- Solidago candensis - Golden Rod
- Lonicera spp - Honeysuckle
- Sedum spectabile - Ice Plant
- Hedera helix - Ivy
- Colchicum autumnale - Meadow Saffron
- Aster novi-belgii - Michaelmas Daisies
- Helianthus spp - Perennial Sunflower
- Centranthus rubra - Red Valerian

Get hold of English Nature leaflets (free!):
'Wildlife-friendly gardening' and
'Wildflower meadows'

Useful websites:
www.back-garden-moths.co.uk
www.nature.ac.uk/browse/591 954.html
www.ukmoths.force9.co.uk
    - rare photo of Orange Upperwing and
      loads of other moths
www.plantswithpurpose.co.uk/wildlife
    - great name for a plant supplier!

Plants to avoid
Non-native plants that most seriously threaten
native plants and their habitats
RHS/Wildlife Trust - www.wildaboutgardens.org

- Quercus ilex - Evergreen Oak
- Robinia pseudoacacia - False Acacia
- Allium paradoxum - Few Flowered Leek
- Impatiens glandulifera - Himalayan Balsam
- Carpobrotus edulis - Hottentot Fig
- Rhododendron ponticum
- Gaultheria shallon - Shallon
- Cotoneaster microphyllus
- Cotoneaster horizontalis
- Hyacinthoides hispanica - Spanish Bluebell

Banned in the UK:
- Heracleum mantegazzianum - Giant Hogweed
- Fallopia japonica - Japanese Knotweed

Plants and parts of plants that provide food
for caterpillars
– from the Field Guide

  Roots of grasses, common nettle, catkins of
sallows and poplar, the unopened buds and
flowers of mature ash, docks, burdocks,
bracken, many herb plants, roots of reeds,
willows, Blackthorn, plum, cherry, hawthorn,
apple, pear, privets, ash, elms, hazel, elder,
oaks, beech, wayfaring tree, lilac and black-
currant, sorrel, common rock rose, knapweed,
heathers, lichens, bilberry, common bird's-foot-
trefoil, meadow vetchling, clover, algae on
stones.

  Refer to Field Guide for more...

Pond

Sunny, sheltered site is good, with some shade during the day. Avoid overhanging trees. Use a butyl rubber lining. Contour sides of the pond to allow frogs and toads to get in and out easily. They need a gently sloping shelf about 20-30cm into the pond. Pond should be at least 60cm at its deepest. Mark an outline with string then dig contours with spade. Remove any sharp objects like stones from the soil. Put down 6cm layer of sand followed by some old carpets, underlay or wetted newspaper before putting the butyl rubber down. Be careful. Make sure it doesn't rip. The amount of liner required is equal to the actual length plus twice the maximum depth, plus 50cm. Add more if I want to make a bog garden. Dig it under the soil around the pond. Put a layer of soil in pond once lined then fill the pond in with a trickle of water. Not a deluge, this will disturb the soil.

Free English Nature booklets

'Dragonflies and Damselflies in Your Garden'
'Garden Ponds and Boggy Areas'
'Amphibians in Your Garden'

Water/bog garden - night-time plants

- Nymphae – Water Lilies (white)
  - Variety Wood White Night
- Chelone – Turtle Head
- Iris sibirica – Siberian or Flag Iris
- Iris ensata – Japanese Flag
- Miscanthus sinensis 'Gracillimus' – Variegated Maiden Grass
- Scirpus tabernemontani 'Zebrinus'
- Typha latifolia 'Variegata'
- Zantedeschia aethiopica – Arum Lily
- Juncus effusus – Soft Rush – reed for dragonflies to perch on

Oxygenators
- Myriophyllum spicatum – Water Milfoil
- Callitriche stagnalis – Water Starwort
- Potamogeton crispus – Curled Pondweed
- Ceratophyllum demersum – Rigid Hornwort

Marginal plants
- Butomus umbellatus – Flowering Rush
- Iris pseudacorus – Yellow Flag

- Menyanthes trifoliata – Bog Bean
- Phalaris arundinacea – Reed Canary Grass
- Caltha palustris – Marsh Marigold

RHS/Wildlife Trust pond plants to avoid
   – www.wildaboutgardens.org
- Hydrocatyle ranunculoides – Floating Pennywort
- Myriophyllum acquaticum – Parrots Feather
- Crassula helmsii – Australian Swamp
                                    Stonecrop
- Azolia filiculoides – Water Fern
- Codium fragile – Green Seafingers
- Lagarosiphon major – Curly Waterweed

Weird frog websites:
www.frogsgalore.com – museum in Wiltshire
www.frognirvana.com

Gardening for hedgehogs
- creating a safe place for over-wintering

- Need a wild area (3m × 1·5m) with plenty of large native plants and a couple of brambles.
- Can make a hibernaculum for winter.
- Could be as easy as a small lean to shelter - place an old board against a wall, fence or other structure and cover it with leaves, compost, soil or branches.
- Or: a bigger metre square log camp. 30-40cm high, packed with dry grass, hay or leaves and covered with a plastic tent-like structure made from tarpaulin type material, which is then buried beneath more logs and leaves to hide the roof and provide insulation. Remember to make an entrance.
- More complicated design at www.spacefornature.co.uk
- Never leave milk for hedgehogs - it gives them diarrhoea. Pet food meat is OK.

   Make sure hedgehogs don't get tangled up in nets in the garden.
   Allow access between gardens.

Gardening for bats
- notes from 'Bats: a guide for gardeners'

Pipistrelle bat population down 70% between 1978 and 1993. Massive reduction in prey due to intensive agriculture, especially the use of pesticides and the practice of removing hedgerows. But also loss of roosting sites in hollow trees.

Things to do
Apparently cats love to hunt bats. Must try and get Mrs Jones to keep her cat in at night during the summer months. Half-an-hour before sunset and then in until the morning. Not known whether bells or sonic collars are effective.

Bat bricks and bat tiles to allow access to cavity walls and roofs — maybe if I get a new roof sometime.

Bat boxes — 11 species of British bat have roosted in bat boxes. Can get up to 40 individuals in a box. If it hasn't been used in 2 years, move it. Fix 15' up in a south-west facing site. Make sure there's a 5' gap beneath and 5' all around to allow easy

flight entry. Attach to tree using tree ties that can be adjusted to take account of future tree growth. If using nails to fix the straps use headless nails to allow the box to be pushed off by tree growth. Use aluminium nails rather than steel if the tree is likely to be felled in the future. Steel nails damage chainsaws. If I want to handle bats must apply for a license from English Nature. Licensing Section, Northminster House, Peterborough PE1 1UA; www.english-nature.org.uk
Do not check bat house between June and mid-August as disturbance may cause bats to abandon young. English Nature produce a booklet, 'Focus on bats'.

Seed mixes and plants:
'The Bats in the Garden Mix'
www.organiccatalogue.com
Also www.nickys-nursery.co.uk and
www.wildflowers.co.uk

Evening and night scented plants

- Dianthus alpinus - Carnation-pink
- Dianthus barbatus - Sweet William
- Filipendula ulmaria - Meadowsweet
- Hesperis matronalis - Dame's Violet/Sweet Rocket
- Linnaea borealis - Twin Flower
- Matthiola longipetala subspecies bicornis - Night scented Stocks
- Phlox
- Primula sikkimensis - Night scented Primrose
- Romneya coulteri - Tree Poppy
- Schizopetalon walkeri - no common name known
- Verbascum - Mullein

Evening and night scented vines

- Clematis rehderiana
- Lonicera sempervirens - Coral Honeysuckle
- Lonicera japonica - Japanese Honeysuckle
- Wisteria floribunda
- Wisteria sinensis

Flowers that open in the evening/night - annuals

- Datura stramonium (reclassified Brugmansia) - Jimson weed/Angels' Trumpets : all parts are highly toxic if ingested
- Dictamnus albus - The Gas Plant - said to emit a gas which can be lit
- Hemerocallis citrina (H. vespertina) - Citrus Day Lily
- Hemerocallis varieties - eenie wenie/gentle shepherd/ joan senior/lullaby baby
- Hesperantha baurii
- Hosta plantaginea - The August Lily or fragrant hosta
- Ipomoea alba - Moonflower
- Lagenaria siceraria - Gourds
- Mirabilis jalapa - Miracle of Peru
- Nicotiana sylvestris - Tobacco Plant
- Oenothera - Evening Primrose
- Saponaria officinalis - Bouncing Bet
- Silene nutans - Nottingham Catchfly
- Zaluzianskya capensis - Night Phlox

White garden – this list could be massive,
some favourites.

- Crocus biflorus
- Digitalis purpurea alba – Foxglove
- Gaura lindheimeri – White Gaura
- Helianthus 'Italian white' – Sunflower
- Nigella damascena alba 'Miss Jekyll' –
  Love in the Mist
- Pelargonium (multibloom series) – Geranium

Check out the RHS Encyclopedia for more.

RHS Top Ten Plants for a night-time garden
www.rhs.org.uk/research/biodiversity/
wildnightout_plants

- Buddleja davidii 'White Profusion' AGM and
'Black Knight' AGM — for dramatic contrast.
- Caryopteris x clandonensis 'First Choice' AGM —
vivid blue flowers from deep indigo buds in summer.
- Cynara cardunculus AGM (globe artichoke) —
loved by moths, creates a striking silhouette
at dusk.
- Eryngium giganteum 'Silver Ghost' AGM — moth
friendly, tiny blue flowers with rosettes of
silvery-grey bracts
- Hebe 'Great Orme' AGM — moth attracting shrub,
small pink to white flowers clustered in dense spikes.
- Jasminum officinale AGM — attracts moths,
glows under moonlight
- Lonicera periclymenum 'Graham Thomas' AGM —
(honeysuckle) white flowers turn to buff yellow
over long flowering season.
- Nicotiana sylvestris AGM — flowering Tobacco
Plant, moth magnet.

- Oenothera fruticosa 'Fyrverkeri' AGM -
                            Evening Primrose
- Verbena bonariensis AGM - grow up to 2m
(6.5ft) high. Attractive to moths. Small purple
flowers.

Digitalis purpurea f.albiflora

As the Middle Ages passed away and humanity began to make the slow transition to a modern understanding of the science of health, the medical profession, and, of course, being tugged along by their enthusiasm, the populus embarked on a craze known as 'The Doctrine of Signatures'. This doctrine suggested that plants that looked like an illness or a part of a body should be used to cure the illness or part of the body it looked like. Thus William Coles used walnuts to cure head ailments, and foxgloves, with their interior-spotted flowers, became the drug of choice to have a crack at spotted lung. We now know that foxgloves have a low therapeutic ratio; which means that the difference in dosage between saving and slaying is small. Take too much of it and you will see your friends, as did Dr John Coakley Lettsom, 'surrounded with a blaze of fire [until] at length [you suffer] almost total blindness.' Grow it to look at instead. The pure white variety (*D. p. f.albiflora*) makes a stunning vision at night, with much of its 1.5m (3-5ft) height covered in tubular bellflowers. Needs partial shade and well-drained soil. It's a biennial and probably won't come true when it sows its seeds. *Albiflora* seeds available from Hall Farm Nursery – www.hallfarmnursery.co.uk.

Tobacco plant (*Nicotiana sylvestris*)

The pure white trumpet-like flowers of the tobacco plant hang down in the style of a low-down blues musician directing his notes to the ground. A moth hoping to retrieve nectar must hang upside down on the lip and use its straw-like proboscis tongue to draw the liquid out. Only those with very long tongues will have success. Although they will open during dull summer days, they long for the night. When it comes they produce what Rosemary Creeser describes as 'a wonderful musky tuberose like fragrance' and Peter Loewer, as a 'sweet scent of freesias'. It is this smell that night flying insects find particularly alluring. If you remember to remove flowers that are past their best they will carry on showing most of the summer and autumn. Prefers a warm sunny spot (although it likes a bit of shade on a hot summer's afternoon). At 1.5m (5ft) tall they are best planted toward the back of a border. This is also better for children, as contact with the leaves may irritate skin. Sow seeds in early spring.

Common jasmine (*Jasminum officinale*)

This is the kind of plant you imagine crept across the door of Sleeping Beauty's cottage as she lay dormant for her prince. It produces a dense snarled mass of braided stems that can spread 3m (10ft) in all directions in just ten years. This is good news for insects and nesting birds, but bad news for the gardener, who must prune each year, after flowering, to avoid both conflict with the neighbours and a rather grubby looking plant. Get rid of old and crowded stems and you will leave plenty of space for fresh stems to produce their distinctive white- or pink-tinctured star-shaped flowers. These will appear from early summer to early autumn and straightaway attract night-time pollinators, as well as butterflies and bees. Grow from semi-ripe cuttings in summer and plant in a sheltered sunny position (such as a south or west facing wall).

Honeysuckle (*Lonicera*)

Grown in sun or shade the honeysuckle family are perfect friends for the night gardener with an awkward plot, although, with its love of moist, slighty acid soils, gardeners in the damp West will find it easiest to grow. Can be grown from seed in autumn or spring, from semi-ripe cuttings in summer or from hardwood cuttings in late autumn. All species provide food and shelter for birds and nectar for moths, but if you are looking for fragrance as well, avoid coral honeysuckle (*Lonicera sempervirens*). Better to go for the common honeysuckle (*Lonicera periclymenum*) or the rigorous sprawling giant Japanese honeysuckle (*Lonicera japonica*) — although this will soon get out of control if left to its own devices. The flowers come from early summer to early autumn but don't prune the flowered wood out until early spring. When you do, take out a third of the oldest flowering shoots back down to ground level.

Evening primrose (*Oenothera*)

If you know someone who will gamble on two flies crossing a ceiling, invite them round to your garden one summer dusk to place a bet on the opening flowers of an evening primrose. These (mostly) yellow (but also pink or red) flowers have fifteen minutes of fame every day when nothing else in the garden should distract your attention. Decide which flower you think will open first and put your wager down. You must be patient though, as the opening can take at least half an hour. At the turn of the last century Neltje Blanchan called these flowers 'ballroom beauties', and it is true that they look their best at dusk and their worst the next day, when their slightly jaded and worn-out appearance mirrors that of a wasted and forlorn partygoer. Dusk is also the best time to see hawk moths feed on their nectar. Need to be planted in full sun (or partial shade in hot areas) in a poor to moderately fertile well-drained soil. They can be sown by seed or dug up from clumps of self-seeded plants in autumn or early spring.

Day lilies (*Hemerocallis*)

There are well over 32,000 cultivars of day lilies registered in the US but not all of them keep their flowers open at night. Cross-referencing Peter Loewer's American book *The Evening Garden* with the Royal Horticultural Society's *Encyclopedia of Plants and Flowers* I have identified at least four that can be classified as night openers and that are available to British gardeners – these are Eenie Weenie, Gentle Shepherd, Joan Senior and Lullaby Baby. There may be more out there but I couldn't vouchsafe their identity. They are, respectively yellow/white/white/pale pink. Using a complicated classification system referenced in *The Evening Garden*, Eenie Weenie is the best out of the four for night-time viewing. Place in full sun or partial shade in fertile, moist soil and this yellow flowering perennial will form a clump of plants reaching a height of 30cm (1ft). It can then be divided in autumn or spring and the divisions planted elsewhere to make new clumps. It flowers in succession in early summer but as its name suggests the flowers last for just one day.

Nottingham catchfly (*Silene nutans*)

So called, as nineteenth century English garden writer Ann Pratt noted, because there were quite a lot of them in Nottingham. If things had been different they might have been called White Cliffs of Dover catchfly, as she saw quite a lot of them there too. The catchfly part of the name refers to their sticky stems thought to catch insects, such as ants, that might steal pollen without helping in fertilization. It has also been called 'sticky cockle'. A more apt and romantic name might be the 'flower of three nights', or 'three times a lady'. Each night at seven, for three nights, the Nottingham catchfly opens its white petals to the darkening summer sky and pumps out a moth magnet of a smell that has been described as 'sweet and reminiscent of hyacinths'. By three the next morning the flower has closed and remains closed until seven the next evening. By the third night, the flower is ready to be fertilized. After that it never opens again. Needs sun and fertile, well-drained soil. Plant seeds in spring or early autumn. Plants supplied by British Wildflower Plants – www.wildflowers.co.uk.

Iris sibirica and Iris ensata

Appropriately, the Greek goddess of the rainbow lends her name to the iris. The eye tends to pick up whites better in moonlit gardens but a carefully placed, low intensity light will bring out the contrasts in those varieties of *Iris sibirica* and *Iris ensata* that have flowers with darker coats. Although there are white *I. sibirica* and *I. ensata* it is more common to find lavenders, violets, purples, oranges and pinks. Monty Don insists that 'no other flower sucks in light so voluptuously and returns it with such velvet intensity of pigment as an iris'. With such a recommendation it would be a shame not to enjoy these tones at night too, especially as the structural arrangement of an iris flower, with its three large drooping petals (falls), three erect standards and three-branched style, is so enchanting. *Iris sibirica* will take to full sun or partial shade and *Iris ensata* to partial shade. Rhizomes must be planted just beneath a moist boggy and poorly drained soil that won't dry up. Their three petals stand for faith, wisdom and valour.

Water lily (*Nymphaea*)

Taking its Latin name from the semi-divine maiden of the sea, a flowering water lily is indeed a celestial sight. At night, the prominent gold stamens of variety 'Wood's White Knight' glow amidst the vessel of creamy white flowers that carry them; each flower shaped like a star and set against mid-green dappled leaves that lie beneath. Leaves that can spread to two feet wide. Each blossom stands above the water's surface and, although an individual blossom lasts just three nights, a plant will bloom all summer given enough sunlight (anything between three and six hours). 'Wood's White Knight' can develop a 2m (6ft) spread, so smaller ponds will benefit from a variety such as 'Emily Grant Hutchings' (1.2m(4ft)) with its bronze-crimson cup flowers, or the aptly named 'Red Flare' (1.5m(5ft)). All these plants are frost tender and need dividing and replanting in spring every 3-4 years. Get rid of old leaves, too, as they can cause water pollution. *Alba*, the native water lily is available from Mimmack Aquatics; 01277 840204.

The August lily or fragrant hosta (*Hosta plantaginea*)

Anyone who wants to see the evening opening, honey-scented, trumpet-shaped white flowers of *Hosta plantaginea* will have to so something about the slugs first. Slugs love the night, too, so you could sniff out slugs and scent at the same time. The older flowers look tired during the day but they find renewed energy at night when they carry on opening for some time. The plant flowers from late summer to early autumn, so it's a good plant to have when the show's nearly over. Peter Loewer records that the Japanese have long appreciated these nocturnal flowers, planting them beside soft, pine needle garden pathways. They can grow to heights of 60cm (2ft) and, in clumps, 1.2m (4ft).

Night-scented stock (*Matthiola longipetala* subspecies *bicornis*)

The pale lilac flowers of the night-scented stock attract lots of night-time pollinators, including the hawk moths (recorded all over Britain from Dover to the Orkneys), with a fragrance reminiscent of almond and vanilla. It can be easily grown from seed pressed into a finely raked soil, but not covered with it, anywhere from early to late spring. Needs sunny, fertile, moist but well drained soil. Because it is prone to various fungal diseases, such as downy mildew and botrytis, night-scented stock must be placed in an open site where air circulation is good. When seedlings are large enough to handle, thin to 8cm (3 inches) apart and always water plants at ground level rather than from above to avoid wetting the leaves.

Meadowsweet (*Filipendula ulmaria*)

The honey-scented plumes of fluffy white flowers that appear on the meadowsweet during the summer months provide one of the most pungent aromas of the night garden. It is a smell that gets heavier as night falls. Garden writer Peter Loewer quotes Richard Jeffries' description of the smell of meadowsweet in his book *The Evening Garden*: 'By day it is pleasant to linger in the meadow and inhale its sweetness. [At night] so heavy and powerful is its odour, the still motionless air between the thick hedges becomes oppressive and it is a relief to issue forth into the open fields from the perfume and the brooding heat.' It loves moist boggy ground (especially around ponds) and is loved by nectar feeding moths and bats, hoverflies and solitary bees, as well as seed eating birds and small mammals. At 2.4m (8ft) *Filipendula rubra* is the queen of the prairie. Keep its nutrient levels up by offering it some leaf mould in the spring.

Mullein (*Verbascum*)

The yellow or white flowers of the mullein only emerge in the second year but, when they do, they create a mass of interest in the garden amongst night-time pollinators as well as a faint but sweet smell. This does not mean that you will yawn at the plant's performance in the first year. It produces silver felted or mid-green leaves that attract (if you live anywhere between Cumbria and the south coast) the larvae of the mullein moth. Aptly named *Verbascum olympicum* it will grow to 1.8m (6ft) but if you don't have room for this mammoth, try one of the smaller varieties such as *Verbascum nigrum* and *Verbascum lychnitis*. It can be grown in poor, well-drained alkaline soil and, although it prefers direct sun, it will tolerate shade. It does need plenty of space, though, as it doesn't like competition. Mullein can be grown from seed in spring or late summer or by root cuttings in winter. When it finishes flowering let the flower heads go to seed: they attract many small garden birds.

Bird cherry (*Prunus padus*)

This is a tree for all seasons but not necessarily all gardens. If left to grow unchecked it will reach 15m (50ft). However, if you have the room to let this tree reach its full potential, you will be rewarded by a grand theatrical performance in four acts, starting with the uncurling of its finely toothed dark green leaves in spring and ending when these leaves turn spectacular shades of red or gold in autumn. In between, there are clusters of almond-scented, cup-shaped white flowers (late spring) and shiny black cherries (summer) to enjoy (though not in an edible sense, as these cherries are strictly for the birds). Even in winter time the dark, reddish-brown, peeling bark provides plenty of interest for the cold eye. It is a great night-time tree. Not only does it carry white flowers, but its leaves are harvested by moth larvae and its flowers pollinated by adult moths. If you want something slightly smaller, Rosemary Creeser also recommends *Prunus virglnia* (10m (30ft)).

Garden Plan Key

Au - Allium ursinum - Wild Garlic
Dp - Digitalis purpurea - Foxglove
Co - Chelone oblique - Turtlehead
He - Hemerocallis - Day Lily
Hm - Hesperis matronalis - Sweet Rocket
Is - Iris siberica - Siberian or Flag Iris
Je - Juncus effuses - Soft Rush
Na - Nymphaen alba - Water Lily
St - Scirpus tabernemontani 'Zebrinus'
Ma - Mentha aquatica - Watermint
Cp - Caltha palustris - Marsh Marigold
Hh - Hedera helix - Common Ivy
Vt - Verbascum - Mullein
Ha - Helianthus - Italian White
Lp - Lonicera - Honeysuckle
Mi - Matthiola longipetala subspecies bicornis -
        Night Scented Stock
Ns - Nicotiana sylvestris - Tobacco Plant
Sn - Silene nutans - Nottingham Catchfly
Ob - Oenothera - Evening Primrose
Da - Dianthus alpinus albus - Carnation
Mj - Mirabilis jalopa - Miracle of Peru
Po - Papaver orientale 'Perry's White' - Poppy
Ls - Lagenaria siceraria - Gourds
Cr - Centranthus rubra alba - white form of
                            Red Valerian
Ss - Sedum spectabile - Iceplant
Lb - Linnaea borealis - Twin Flower
Jo - Jasminum officinale - Common Jasmine

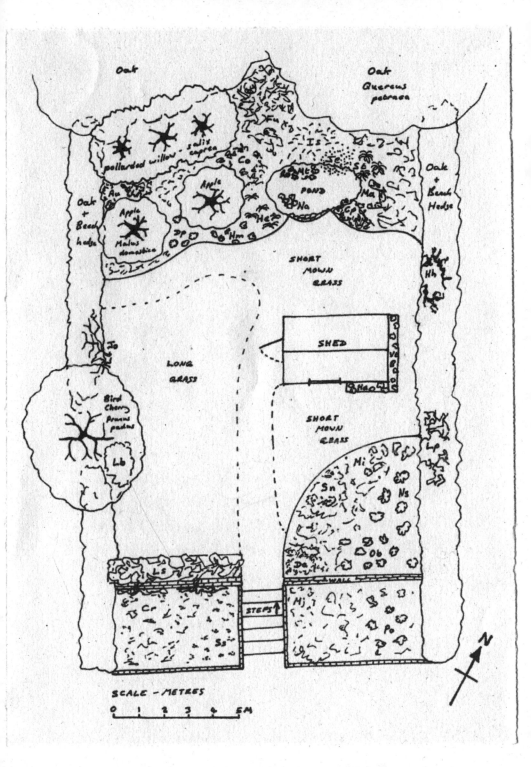

Notes on lighting

Been reading a lot about lighting in the garden. One book suggests enough light to mimic the moon or prevent tripping, stumbling or stubbing a toe. I think I have three main options.

Random lighting
• Option One. Flexible. Changes depending on the occassion. A few candles and a torch. Allow the garden to be mainly lit by the moon. Enjoy the contrasts the different levels of moonlight give, from no moon, to slither, to full. Some nights are best just sitting under the stars with no lights, or perhaps one or two tea lights. I have a couple of old tins punctured with holes I bought at Glastonbury and two 1950s paraffin holders I found at the recycling yard and cut holes in for candles. Must look at that book 'The Art of the Tin Can' for other ideas. Would be nice to have a small, contained fire area as well.

• Option Two. Fixed Lighting. Don't make a big deal of it. Just have a few solar path markers from www.cat.org.uk, a solar pond light maybe. Dot them around the garden just to give some safe low level lighting that allows me to move about freely without worrying about torches and candles.

• Option Three. Design the lighting. Make a plan of the garden, assess where I want the lighting, which plants I want to light up and how I want them lit, from above, beneath, the side, and with what intensity – dim, medium or bright. Whether I want the emphasis on shadowing. Or silhouetting. Or diffuse lighting. The best way to do this, I reckon, is to go off with a load of different sized candles and move them around the garden. Also use torches of various powers. My bike light's definitely much brighter than the others. Make a plan of the garden and draw on what I want, where I want it. Then either get an electrician in to do the work laying cables, or buy solar. Work out which is cheaper, most convenient and delivers the lighting I want.

NB. Must switch to green electricity.
Check out www.foe.co.uk for more info.

Lighting suppliers
- Creations Artistic Ironsmiths - unusual and interesting artifacts:
  49-53 South Street, Bishops Stortford, Herts, CM23 3AG; 01279 658355; www.ukcreations.co.uk
- Clearlight - outdoor candle suppliers:
  London House, Lynn Road, Grayton, Kings Lynn, Norfolk, PE32 1QJ; www.clearlight.uk.net
- Glenn Stephenson - hand painted lanterns:
  The Pixie in the Willow
  pixiewillow@aol.com; 07713 558161

Websites for night lights
- www.cat.org.uk - range of solar lights, including firefly shape
- www.go1better.co.uk/Garden/Lighting/2 - torch oil and blow torch cylinder lights...

beautiful perhaps but environmentally
wasteful
- www.impactlighting.com - standard low
  voltage lighting suppliers
- www.garden-nut.co.uk - butterfly-shaped
  fairy lights
- www.just-candles.net
- www.homefarmcandles.co.uk - hand-made
  flares
- www.st-eval-candle.co.uk/candle - hand-made
  stylish outdoor candles
- www.hurricanelamps.co.uk

(Chimineas for a contained fire - also hammocks)
- www.hammocks.co.uk - fair trade Mexican
  products including chimineas, ponchos and
  very big hammocks and hammock stands

- Also look at www.handmadehammocks.co.uk

Ways to attract moths to count

www.angleps.btinternet.co.uk –
Free beginners' guide to moth trapping on
their website. Read before using a light trap.
Lots of good tips. Best nights are cloudy,
warm and dark. Full moons reduce catch.
As do cold clear nights. Strong winds reduce
success rate and blow traps over.

Sugar traps – Nick Baker suggests a mixture
of sugar, molasses, fruit juices and dark
rum heated gently in a pan. It should be
runny enough to use as a paint but not so
runny it dribbles on the ground. Once made,
pour in a jam jar and apply generously to
eye level to between ten and twenty tree
trunks and fence posts with a paintbrush.
Or make a runnier mixture and pour over
old rags. Check for moths by torchlight for
the first two hours of darkness. The field
guide suggests black treacle with a dash of
rum or beer. Or sour chutney and over ripe

bananas.

Recipe from Butterfly Conservation -

454g tin of black treacle, 1kg brown sugar, 500ml brown ale or cola or Irn Bru - slowly heat ale in a large pan and simmer for five mins. Stir in and dissolve the sugar, followed by the treacle and then simmer for two mins. Allow to cool before pouring into a container.

Or a 1m length of rope soaked in a saturated solution of red wine and white sugar. Hang from trees, bushes or fences just before dusk and check for moths by torch-light for the first two hours of darkness. Recipe: bottle of cheap red wine, 1kg sugar. Heat the wine and stir in the sugar until dissolved.

Light traps - A sheet can be hung from a line with a bulb suspended above it. The moths will rest on the sheet. In windy conditions lay a sheet on the ground and place a light on top of it. Commercially bought traps: Mercury Vapour Discharge Bulbs, Robinson,

Skinner and Heath. Get from:
Anglian Lepidopterist Supplies
01263 862068; www. angleps. btinternet. co.uk

Build your own light trap — guide at:
www. atropos. info — should cost no more than
£40.

National Status and Conservation categories

- Red Data Book - species known from 15 or fewer 10km squares in Britain since 1980
- Nationally Scarce A - recorded from 16-30 10km squares since 1980
- Nationally Scarce B - recorded from 31-100 10km squares since 1980
- Local - recorded from 101-300 10km squares since 1960
- Common - recorded from over 300 10km squares since 1960
- Immigrant - flown or transported by wind from outside Britain
- Import - Imported in goods
- Doubtfully British - unsubstantiated reports

Possible effects of climate change on moths

Starvation – Food source can be wiped out by storms or disease brought about by drought or flood. Many species of moth match their life cycle to the arrival of certain types of food. This is a trick learnt over thousands of generations. Many indicators say that spring is arriving earlier and winter later. Many plants, reacting to temperature increases, are flowering earlier. Moths may not be able to adapt quickly enough to the new cycles and may miss out on food sources.

Freak weather events – High winds can blow larvae from their food plants. Adult moths can be blown out to sea. Blossom can be blown more easily off trees, reducing nectar sources. Sheltered areas become more important. Hedgerows and woodland shelter belts. Unseasonal heavy rain or hail may cause injury or death to moths. If they are grounded in a puddle they find it very difficult to break the surface tension of the water. I quite often find moths in puddles after storms. Severe flooding may cause heavy mortality to larvae that feed or over-winter in low herbage or within feed stems. Also leads to fungal attack.

New competitors - Changes in temperature in Britain are already leading to the arrival of domineering species of wildlife, such as a new species of ladybird identified in 2004. These have evolved to cope with different environments and can be tougher than native species. British moths will head north as the temperatures go up but no one is sure how long their temperature range will last.

Disease pathogens - viruses, bacteria, ultra-selfish symbionts, fungi, protozoa - new strains might develop with hotter temperatures.

Butterflies move north in Europe

Study published in the journal 'Nature'.
Of 35 species capable of moving in response to
climate factors 63% had shifted north by
35-240 km in the twentieth century.
The average temperature increase in Europe in
the same period was 0.8 degrees Celsius,
shifting climactic isotherms northwards
by 120 km. Future predicted temperature rises
vary between 2.1-4.6 degrees Celsius.

Notes on global warming and extinction
Study published in the science journal 'Nature'
Between 15% and 37% of species could be lost
in the next 50 years if we can't control man-
made global warming. 18 scientists from
around the world took a cross section of
1,103 species from five regions that encompass
20% of the Earth's surface, including Europe,
Australia, Mexico, Brazil and South Africa,
and married the projected climate change in
particular regions with maps describing the

habitat – especially the climate needs – of plants and animals in the same area. They found that we will be committing 1·25 million species to extinction.

Up to six degrees of warming is now predicted by the Intergovernmental Panel on Climate Change (IPCC) in the next 100 years. Researchers at Bristol University have shown that 6 degrees of warming was enough to wipe out 95% of species at the end of the Permian period 252 million years ago.

Notes on man made carbon emissions and global warming

Since the Industrial Revolution global atmospheric concentration of CO_2 has increased from 220 parts per million to 370 parts per million. A 2 degree rise in temperature is predicted if the amount of man made CO_2 in the ~~atmosphere~~ atmosphere rises to 450 parts per million. If current trends continue we will reach this figure within the next fifty years. Temperature rises over two degrees will lead to long lasting damage to temperature regulating eco-systems such as the Amazon rainforest. Runaway global warming is possible if we do nothing about our carbon emissions. Already the frozen wastes of Siberia are defrosting, threatening to release into the atmosphere vast quantities of methane currently trapped in permafrost. Methane is a much more deadly global warming gas than CO_2. Predicted temperature rises are between 2 degrees Celcius and 10 degrees

Celcius. The last time the Earth suffered such a large temperature increase it took 60,000 years for temperatures to stabilise again. No one really knows what effect such a temperature increase will have on humans but large scale migrations have been predicted as people flee areas which ~~will be~~ become inhospitable, either because of excessive flooding or drought, soil erosion and famine. Loss of food, water and other vital resources will lead to increased mortality. So called natural disasters will displace people, create panic and destabilise economies.

Notes from 'A Short History of Nearly Everything' by Bill Bryson

We only have to look at Venus, where the sun's warmth arrives just two minutes before it reaches Earth to see how lucky we are. It is thought that Venus was only slightly warmer than Earth when the solar system emerged from the catastrophic explosion that created it. It had vast seas just like Earth but couldn't hold on to its surface water because it was too hot. The hydrogen atoms evaporated into space leaving oxygen atoms to combine with carbon to form the greenhouse gas carbon dioxide. The surface temperature on Venus is now 470 degrees Celcius.

How much is the planet worth?
Notes from 'The Future of Life' by Edward O.
Wilson

Eco-systems services provided to humanity
free of charge by the living natural environment - estimated in 1997 as $33 trillion or
more each year - almost twice the 1997
combined Gross National Product (GNP) of all
the countries in the world.
Eco-system services are defined as the flow
of materials, energy and information from
the biosphere that support human existence.
They include the regulation of the atmosphere
and climate; the purification and retention
of fresh water; the formation and the
enrichment of the soil; nutrient cycling; the
detoxification and recirculation of waste;
the pollination of crops; and the production
of lumber, fodder and biomass fuel.
If humanity were to try to replace the
free services of the natural economy with
substitutes of its own manufacture, the GNP

would have to be raised by at least
$33 trillion. An economic and physical
impossibility.

No one can guess the future value of any
kind of animal, plant or micro-organism.
Its potential is spread across a spectrum of
know and as yet unimagined human needs.

In the US about one-quarter of all
prescriptions are substances extracted from
plants.

Another 13% originate from micro-organisms
and 3% more from animals.

Nine of the ten leading prescription drugs
originally came from organisms. Their
value - $84 billion worldwide.

List of drugs from plants and animals:
antibiotics, fungicides, anti-malarial drugs,
anaesthetics, analgesics, blood thinners,
blood clotting agents, agents that prevent
clotting, cardiac stimulants and regulators,
immuno-suppressive agents, hormone mimics,
hormone inhibitors, anti-cancer drugs, fever
suppressants, inflammation controls,

contraceptives, anti-depressants and
muscle relaxants.

Endlings
All taken from 'A Gap in Nature', except 'Turgie
the snail' from 'The Future of Life'.

Great Auk, 1844, Eldey (Iceland)
    Harried to extinction by explorers and
fishermen, the last few remained on a small
volcanic outcrop off the coast of Iceland. When
this disappeared into the sea after an eruption,
the few remaining birds moved to Eldey. On
3rd June, 1844, a party of sailors clubbed the
final pair to death to sell the bodies to a
collector. The eggs they were sitting on were
crushed under foot.

Passenger Pigeon, 1914, USA
    At one point the passenger pigeon accounted
for four North American birds out of ten. Last
passenger pigeon died in Cincinnati Zoo on the
first day of September, 1914.

Carolina Parakeet, 1918, Eastern North America
   An anomaly in the world; a rare northern
hemisphere parrot whose territory spread as
far north as the great lakes. Last Carolina
Parakeet died in Cincinnati Zoo on either the
14th or 21st February, 1918.

Thylacine, 1936, Tasmania
   Wolf shaped predator of marsupial. Blessed
with beautiful fur, they were hunted into
extinction. The last Thylacine was kept in
Beaumaris Zoo, 'exposed both night and day
in an open, wire-topped cage, with no access
to its sheltered den.' Extreme weather exposed
her to freezing night-time temperatures and
soaring heat during the day. Ignored by her
keepers, she died on the 7th September, 1936.

Toolache Wallaby, 1939, Australia
   Legendary for their speed, the were hunted
for fur or sport. The last Toolache Wallaby
was taken from the wild in 1927 and lived in

captivity at Robe on the South Australian
coast for twelve years. She died in the
winter of 1939.

Partulina turgida, January, 1996, Moorea
   Extinguished in the wild by rosy wolf-
snails, a predatory snail introduced to the
island to control other snails. Partulina
turgida evolved 1·5 million years ago. Turgie
the snail died at London Zoo in January 1996,
after ten years of unsuccessful conservation
attempts.

Geological periods

4,600 million years ago – 550 million years
                        Pre-Cambrian Eon

543 – 490 million years ago – Cambrian
490 – 443 million years ago – Ordovician
443 – 418 million years ago – Silurian
418 – 354 million years ago – Devonian
354 – 290 million years ago – Carboniferous
290 – 252 million years ago – Permian
252 – 199.5 million years ago – Triassic
199.5 – 142 million years ago – Jurassic
142 – 65 million years ago – Cretaceous
65 – 1.8 million years ago – Tertiary
1.8 million years ago – present day – Quaternary

Time Line - evolution and extinction

- Earth born - 4,600 million years ago
- Ordovician/Silurian extinction event - 440 million years ago : 50% of marine genera wiped out
- First upright land plant - 430 million years ago
- First wingless insects and composters (spiders, mites, pseudoscorpions) - 405 million years ago
- First tree like plants - 380 million years ago
- Devonian extinction event - 368 million years ago
- Permian/Triassic extinction event - 252 million years ago : 60% of marine & terrestrial genera wiped
- First flies - 225 million years ago
- Triassic/Jurassic extinction event - 200 million years ago
- First birds - 150 million years ago
- First flowering-plant pollen - 135 million years ago
- KT extinction event - 65 million years ago
- First primate - 65 million years ago
- Spread of song birds - 20 million years ago
- First cattle, spread of snakes, frogs, rats and mice - 14 million years ago
- Earliest human relatives - 7 million years ago
- Homo habilis - 2.5 million years ago (fossil)

- Homo erectus - 1.8 million years ago (fossil)
- Homo antecessor - 0.8 million years ago (fossil)
- Homo neanderthalensis / Homo heidelbergensis -
         0.3 million years ago (fossil)
- Homo sapiens - between 465,000 and 260,000 years
         ago (according to DNA), 130,000 years
         ago (fossil)

Homo sapiens – extinction event : 50,000 years ago
to present day

"The vital spark from inanimate matter to animate life happened once... all living existence depends on that moment. We are one tribe with bacteria that live in hot springs, parasitic barnacles, vampire bats and cauliflowers."
Richard Fortey

"The most memorable heritage of the twenty-first century will be the Age of Loneliness that lies before humanity."
Edward O. Wilson

"As if you could kill time without injuring eternity."
Henry David Thoreau

References

References and Latin names for flora and fauna noted in the text:

1. Orange Upperwing - *Jodia croceago*
2. Common ivy - *Hedera helix*
3. Honeysuckle – *Lonicera* (in variety)
4. Common jasmine - *Jasminum officianale*
5. Cambrian poppy - *Meconopsis cambrica*
6. Gourds - *Lagenaria siceraria*
7. Bird cherry - *Prunus padus*
8. White foxgloves - *Digitalis purpurea f.albiflora*
9. Twin flower - *Linnaea borealis*
10. Wild garlic - *Allium ursinum*
11. Sweet rocket - *Hesperis matronalis*
12. Day lily – *Hemerocallis* (in variety)
13. Eyed Hawkmoth - *Smerinthus ocellata*
14. Walnut spider - *Nuctenea umbratica*
15. Crab spider - *Xysticus cristatus*
16. Swallowtailed moth - *Ourapteryx sambucaria*
17. *Phalera bucephala/Orgyia antiqua/Miltochrista miniata/Arctia caja*
18. Evening primrose – *Oenothera* (in variety)
19. Heart And Dart - *Agrotis exclamationis*

Flora and fauna mentioned in the Memory Book

Water lily - *Nymphae* (variety: Wood's White Knight)
Watermint - *Mentha aquatica*
White poppies - *Papaver orientale* (variety: Perry's White)
Nottingham Catchfly - *Silene nutans*
Sunflower - *Helianthus* (variety: Italian white)
Woodlouse spiders - *Dysdera crocata*

The original story about chimpanzees staring at the sunset was reported in an article by Adrian Kortlandt in *Scientific American*.

Organisations

- Amateur Entomologists' Society,
  PO Box 8774, London SW7 5ZG;
  www.theaes.org – great for beginners
- Atropos Magazine – for free sample send sae with 54p stamp
  to 36 Tinker Lane, Meltham, Holmfirth, West Yorkshire HD9
  4EX
- The Bat Conservation Trust,
  15 Cloisters House, 8 Battersea Park Road, London SW8
  4BG; Tel: 020 7627 2629; www.bats.org.uk.
- British Arachnological Society,
  Membership Treasurer, 71 Havant Road, Walthamstow,
  London E17 3EJE; www.britishspiders.org.uk
- British Hedgehog Preservation Society, Hedgehog House,
  Dhustone, Ludlow, Shropshire SY8 3PL; Tel: 01584 890801;
  www.software technics.com/bhps
- Buglife – The Invertebrate Conservation Trust, 170A Park
  Road, Peterborough, Cambridgeshire PE21 2UF;
  Tel: 01733 201210; www.buglife.org.uk
- Butterfly Conservation, Manor Yard, East Lulworth,
  Wareham, Dorset BH20 5QP; Tel: 0870 774 4309;
  www.butterfly-conservation.org
- English Nature, Northminster House,
  Peterborough PE7 0LG; www.english-nature.org.uk
- Friends of the Earth, 26-28 Underwood Street,
  London N1 7JQ; 0207 490 0881; www.foe.co.uk

- Froglife, White Lodge, London Road,
  Peterborough PE7 0LG; Tel: 01733 558844; www.froglife.org
- HDRA Organic Gardens, Yalding, Benover Road, Yalding,
  Near Maidstone, Kent ME18 6EX;
  Tel: 01622 814650; www.hdra.org.uk
- The Hawk and Owl Trust, 11 St Mary's Close, Abbotskerswell,
  Newton Abbot, Devon TQ12 5QF; Tel: 01626 334864;
  www.hawkandowl.org
- Ponds Conservation Trust, BMS, Oxford Brookes University,
  Gipsy Lane, Headington, Oxford OX3 0BP; Tel: 01865 483249
- Royal Society for the Protection of Birds (RSPB), The Lodge,
  Sandy, Bedfordshire SG19 2DL; Tel: 01767 680551;
  www.rspb.org.uk

The night-time garden at Glastonbury was inspired by the work of Jenny and Mehdi. Jenny and Mehdi specialise in holistic design and the creation of soulful spaces using environmentally conscious materials. Email jennyandmehdi@yahoo.com or visit www.jennyandmehdi.org to see examples of their work.

Mail Order

- Anglian Lepidopterist Supplies, Station Road, Hindolveston, Norfolk NR20 5DE; Tel: 01263 862068; www.angleps.btinternet.co.uk
- British Wild Flower Plants, Burlingham Gardens, 31 Main Road, North Burlingham, Norfolk NR13 4TA; Tel: 01603 716615; www.wildflowers.co.uk
- Centre for Alternative Technology, Machynlleth, Powys, SY20 9AZ; Tel: 01654 705959; www.cat.org.uk wide range of books, solar lights, wind up torches, bird and bat boxes, bee houses and natural pest controls.
- Hall Farm Nursery, Vicarage Lane, Kinnerley, Nr. Oswestry, Shropshire SY10 8DH; Tel: 01691 682135; www.hallfarmnursery.co.uk
- Natural History Book Service, 2-3 Wills Road, Totnes, Devon TQ9 5XN; Tel: 01803 865913; www.nhbs.com
- Nickys Seeds, Fairfield Road, Broadstairs, Kent, CT10 2JU; Tel: 01843 600972; www.nickys-nursery.co.uk/seeds
- The Organic Catalogue, Chase Organics, River Dene Business Park, Molesey Road, Hersham, Surrey KT12 4RG; Tel: 0845 130 134; www.organiccatalog.com
- Wiggly Wigglers, Lower Blakemere Farm, Blakemere, Herefordshire HR2 9PX; Tel: 01981 500391; www.wigglywigglers.co.uk
- Small Life Supplies, Station Buildings, Station Road, Bottesford, Nottinghamshire NG13 0EB; www.small-life.co.uk

- The English Cottage Garden Nursery, Herons, Giggers Green Road, Aldington, Kent TN25 7BU; Tel: 01233 720907; www.englishplants.co.uk
- The Microscope Shop, Oxford Road, Sutton Scotney, Winchester, Hants SO21 3RG
- Watkins and Doncaster the Naturalists, PO Box 5, Cranbrook, Kent TN18 5EZ; Tel: 01580 753133; www.watdon.com

Bibliography

Moths, bats, butterflies and other wonders

An Obsession with Butterflies, Sharman Art Russell, Arrow Books, 2004

Bats, Phil Richardson, Smithsonian Institution Press/Natural History Museum, 2002

Bats: a guide for gardeners, Fiona Mathews, Osmia Publications, 2004

Butterflies, Jean-pierre Vesco and Paul Starosta, Hachette Illustrated, 2004

Discover Nature at Sundown, Elizabeth P. Lawlor, Stackpole Books, 1995

Fauna Britannica, Stefan Buczacki, Hamlyn, 2002

Field Guide to the Moths of Great Britain and Ireland, Paul Waring, Martin Townsend and Richard Lewington, British Wildlife Publishing, 2003

How to Attract Butterflies to your Garden, John and Maureen Tampion, Guild of Master Craftsman Publications, 2003

Love Among the Butterflies: The diaries of a wayward, determined and passionate Victorian Lady, Margaret Fountaine, Penguin Books, 1980

Moths, Michael Majerus, The New Naturalist Library, Harper Collins, 2002

Spiders in the Garden, Dr Rod Preston-Mafham, Osmia Publications Ltd, 2003

RSPB Bird Guide, Mullarney et al, HarperCollins, 1999

The Encyclopedia of Insects and Invertebrates, Burton and
Burton, Silverdale Books, 2002
The Encyclopedia of Animals, Burton and Burton, Silverdale
Books, 2002
The New Amateur Naturalist, Nick Baker, Collins, 2004

Evolution and extinction

A Gap in Nature: Discovering the world's extinct animals, Tim
Flannery and Peter Schouten, William Heinemann, 2001
A Short History of Nearly Everything, Bill Bryson, Black
Swan, 2003
*Acquainted with the Night: Excursions through the world after
dark*, Christopher Dewdney, Bloomsbury, 2004
*Dr Tatiana's Sex Advice to all Creation: The Definitive Guide
to the Evolutionary Biology of Sex*, Olivia Judson, Vintage,
2003
Earth, James F.Luhr, Dorling Kindersley/Ted Smart, 2003
Evolution: The triumph of an idea, from Darwin to DNA, Carl
Zimmer, Arrow Books, 2003
Extinction, Evolution and the End of Man, Michael Boulter,
4th Estate, 2002
H2O - A Biography of Water, Philip Ball, Phoenix, 2004
*Life, An Unauthorised Biography: A Natural History of the
first 4,000,000,000 Years of Life on Earth*, Richard Fortey,
Flamingo, 1998
*Sex, Botany and Empire: the story of Carl Linnaeus and
Joseph Banks*, Patricia Fara, Icon Books, 2003
The Future of Life, Edward O. Wilson, Abacus, 2002
The Song of the Dodo, David Quammen, Hutchinson, 1996
The New York Public Library Science Desk Reference, Patricia
Barnes-Svarney, Macmillan, 1995

The garden

Botanical Latin, William T Stearn, David and Charles, 2004
Chris Packham's Back Garden Nature Reserve, The Wildlife Trusts, New Holland, 2001
Dangerous Garden: The quest for plants to change our lives, David Stuart, Frances Lincoln, 2004
Ecology For Gardeners, Steven B.Carroll and Steven D.Salt, Timber Press, 2004
Illustrations of the British Flora, W H Fitch and W G Smith, L Reeve and Co, 1892
Food for Free, Richard Mabey, Fontana/Collins, 1975
Perfect Plant, Perfect Place, Roy Lancaster, Ted Smart, 2001
Science and the Garden: The Scientific basis of horticultural practice, David S. Ingram, Daphne Vince Prue and Peter J. Gregory, Royal Horticultural Society and Blackwell Publishing, 2002
The Complete Gardener, Monty Don, Dorling Kindersley, 2003
The Evening Garden: Flowers and fragrance from dusk till dawn, Peter Loewer, Timber Press, 1993
The Royal Horticultural Society Encyclopedia of Plants and Flowers, Christopher Brickell, Dorling Kindersley, 2004
The Royal Horticultural Society Encyclopedia of Herbs, Deni Brown, Dorling Kindersley, 1995
Weeds, Friend or Foe?: An illustrated guide to identifying, taming and using weeds, Sally Roth, Carroll and Brown Publishers Ltd, 2001
Wildlife Friendly Plants, Rosemary Creeser, Collins and Brown, 2004

Other inspirations

The Curious Incident of the Dog at Night-time, Mark Haddon,
Vintage, 2004
The Little Prince, Antoine de Saint-Exupery, Mammoth, 1991
To Kill a Mockingbird, Harper Lee, Arrow, 2000
Walden, Henry David Thoreau, Princeton University Press,
2004
It's A Wonderful Life, Frank Capra, 1946

Other books by Allan Shepherd published by the Centre for Alternative Technology:

The Little Book of Garden Heroes, 2004
52 Weeks to Change Your World, with Caroline Oakley, 2003
How to Make Soil and Save Earth, 2003
The Little Book of Slugs, with Suzanne Galant, 2002

Other gardening books from the Centre for Alternative Technology:

Creative Sustainable Gardening, Diana Anthony, 2000
'No matter how cunning an organic gardener you are, this book is sure to teach you something. Read it if you can.'
Garden Answers

For details of our full range of 80 titles visit
www.cat.org.uk/catpubs